You Haven't Failed
You Just Haven't Finished...
YET!

by Shawn M. Condra

Copyright © 2024 Shawn M. Condra. All rights reserved.

ISBN: 979-8-218-48335-7

No part of this book may be reproduced, distributed, or transmitted in any form or by any means, including photocopying, recording, or other electronic or mechanical methods, without the prior written permission of the publisher, except in the case of brief quotations embodied in critical reviews and certain other noncommercial uses permitted by copyright law.

"To my wife, Stephany, and our daughters, Lillian and Abigail. Thank you for showing me that true success is measured by the moments we share and the joy we create together."

Contents

Introduction 1

Chapter 1: The Starting Line 5

Chapter 2: The 80/20 Challenge 9

Chapter 3: Ideas Without Action 19

Chapter 4: Silencing the Fear Within 33

Chapter 5: The Landscape of Limitations 47

Chapter 6: The Resilient Path 59

Chapter 7: Embracing the Journey 73

Chapter 8: The "Yet Mindset" 83

Chapter 9: Start the Finish 93

Closing Statement 101

Reflective Exercises 103

About the Author 107

Introduction

"I've failed…" Have you ever had that thought lingering in the back of your mind, or caught yourself saying those words? It's important to understand that you are not alone in these moments. We've all been there, standing at the crossroads of doubt. Maybe that venture you poured your heart into didn't pan out, or that brilliant idea you had, somehow remained in the shadows. And there might have been that time you dedicated yourself to something, only to find an unexpected turn in the path. But here's the thing: it's not just you. We all face these twists and turns, and every hiccup, every detour, holds a lesson waiting to be discovered.

Pause for a second and take a deep breath. Allow your mind to journey back to that special moment, the one that felt like an electric jolt coursing through your veins. Can you feel it? That undeniable, stimulating rush of excitement? It's as if every fiber of your being resonated with the certainty that you were on to something big, a breakthrough.

Those early days were so rich with promise. Your mind was a whirlwind, bursting with ideas, visions, and plans. It wasn't just about the end goal but the exciting feeling that you were on the edge of something great. There was this vivid, nearly clear image of success in your mind's eye, a future so bright and so close you could almost touch it.

Now, let's journey a bit further, to a point in time that might be a bit harder to recollect. Days turned to weeks, weeks to months, and even years rolled on for some. Remember that moment when it felt like the walls of your perfectly built castle started to crumble? That indescribable sting when something you were fully convinced about, so passionately committed to, didn't pan out the way you envisioned?

Recall that sensation, but only for a moment. The weight of disappointment pressing against your chest, the echoing whispers of doubt creeping into your mind. Perhaps you labeled yourself a 'failure' or, even more piercing, heard it from the lips of others. Those cutting words and challenging moments are not easy to face, but they are fundamental. They shape and mold us, and even though they seem like setbacks, they pave the path for the most significant comebacks.

If you take one thing away from this book, let it be this. "You haven't failed." Say it out loud to yourself.

I HAVEN'T FAILED!

The truth is you haven't failed. You've merely paused. This book isn't about facing the idea of incompletion, but rather one of continuation. Together, we will embark on a journey of what got you to where you are now and how you can move forward to finish what you started. True failure only happens when you give up. To quote Thomas Edison, "Our greatest weakness lies in giving up. The most certain way to succeed is always to try just one more time." You owe it to yourself to try just one more time.

> *"Our greatest weakness lies in giving up. The most certain way to succeed is always to try just one more time."*
>
> **Thomas Edison**

Let's step back to that special moment from earlier. Hold on to those initial feelings, that deep-seated passion and energy. It's an integral part of who you are. These memories, these feelings, they're not just passing moments; they're powerful reminders. They're indicators of your drive, ambition, and dormant potential, waiting to be unleashed once more. Remember, every significant endeavor starts with that single, charged thought. Embrace it, and let it guide you forward.

Invitation to the Journey

As we move forward, I invite you to embark on a transformative journey. This is not just any journey, but a journey of self-discovery and overcoming, where I will guide you through the intricate pathways of personal growth and resilience. In the pages ahead, we will explore the forces and decisions that have shaped where you stand today, and together, we will navigate the waters of overcoming obstacles and setbacks.

As your guide, I bring you theories, real-life experiences, and practical wisdom. My role is to illuminate the possibilities that lie ahead, to help you see beyond the immediate challenges, and to discover the untapped potential within you. This journey is about finding the courage to face what has been holding you back and embracing the opportunities that await you.

Consider this book a roadmap that leads you through the valleys of doubt and the peaks of achievement. As you turn each page, you'll find strategies to overcome the hurdles that have slowed your progress and insights to help you understand your journey's context.

So, as we step up to the starting line, approach it with an open mind and a willing heart. Be ready to confront the truths about your journey, to question, to reflect, and to grow. My hope for you is that by the time you reach the end of this book, you will have a clearer understanding of where you've been, where you stand, and most importantly, how you can move forward to where you want to be.

Welcome to your journey – a journey to rediscover yourself, overcome, and succeed.

Chapter 1:
The Starting Line

Every monumental journey starts with a single, often small, yet vital spark – an idea. While unique in its specifics, this spark is a universal experience shared by all who dare to dream and aspire. It's that moment when possibility takes root, and the ordinary can transform into the extraordinary.

Take, for instance, my first endeavor into the world of business at the age of 18. Fueled by youthful enthusiasm and a desire to carve my own path, I ventured into what I believed was a promising business opportunity. The idea was bright, filled with potential, and it felt like the beginning of something significant. However, the journey that followed wasn't quite what I had envisioned. Like many first attempts, the venture encountered its share of hurdles and did not turn out as I had hoped. This experience, though not unique to me, is a testament to the unpredictable nature of acting on a spark.

You might recall similar moments in your life. Think back to when you first experienced that 'spark' – perhaps it was a business idea, a creative project, or a personal goal. It might have come to you in a flash of insight or as a growing realization. Regardless of its nature, that initial spark likely filled you with a mix of excitement and apprehension. It represented possibility – a departure from the routine, a step into a new realm of potential.

Your spark, like mine, might not have led to immediate success or may have veered off in unexpected directions.

But it's important to recognize that these early experiences, these first ventures into the unknown, are not just about the outcomes they generate. They are, more importantly, about the journey they initiate – a journey of discovery, learning, and growth.

First Steps

Embarking on a new venture or pursuing a long-held dream often begins with optimism and determination. When I took my first steps toward my goals, I was propelled by excitement and a bold vision for the future. However, what often isn't anticipated in those initial stages are the challenges that inevitably arise. These unexpected and often overwhelming challenges are an integral part of the journey.

In my case, stepping into my first business venture at 18, I was quickly confronted with my own challenges. With no real business knowledge, I struggled to create a plan, manage finances, and maintain confidence in my decisions. Every step felt uncertain, but these obstacles became valuable learning experiences, teaching me that the journey to achieving goals is rarely straightforward but instead demands resilience, adaptability, and a willingness to learn from each setback.

As you reflect on your own 'first steps,' it's important to remember that encountering challenges is a universal experience. Whether it's the struggle to find the right direction, the battle to overcome personal insecurities, or the challenge of resource limitations, these are common threads in the tapestry of pursuing our ambitions. The roadblocks and detours you've faced or are currently facing have been encountered by many others on their paths to success.

Understanding that these early challenges are not signs of failure or poor judgment is important. They play a key role in shaping who you become and building the strength, knowledge, and perseverance necessary for future success. Taking that first step toward a goal is an act of courage, and the obstacles that follow are what help strengthen your skills and shape your character.

Navigating Early Challenges

As we proceed from this starting line, it's important to understand the nature of early challenges and how to navigate them. Each challenge you face is an opportunity to build perseverance, preparing you for greater obstacles and opportunities ahead.

Consider these early challenges as your personal training ground. They test your resolve, creativity, and adaptability. For example, when I faced financial constraints in my first business, I had to learn the art of resourcefulness. When self-doubt crept in, I had to build my confidence and find ways to stay motivated.

The key is to view these challenges not as barriers but as essential experiences that contribute to your growth. Every obstacle overcome adds to your skill set, making you more resilient and capable of handling future hurdles.

Now, let's take that first step and get ready to embark on your journey.

Chapter 2: The 80/20 Challenge

Embarking on any new venture or project often starts with an unmistakable surge of enthusiasm, a phenomenon that aligns closely with the Pareto Principle. This principle suggests that most of the results often stem from a relatively minor portion of the effort. I have encountered this many times in my career, where the initial stages of a project unfolded with surprising ease and efficiency.

One such example from my experience dates to 2005 while working on an associate's degree in computer information systems. My final project was ambitious: creating a Point of Sale (POS) application that interfaced with a PDA, enabling servers in restaurants to take orders directly at the table. At that time, nothing available in the market offered such a capability. The project was a resounding success academically, earning me an A for its innovation and execution.

However, the real challenge emerged post-completion. Despite the project's potential and its relevance in a rapidly evolving tech landscape, the journey from a successful academic project to a marketable product proved overwhelming. I found myself at a crossroads, equipped with an innovative idea but uncertain about the next steps. This uncertainty and lack of direction halted my progress completely.

My experience mirrors the essence of the 80/20 rule - while creating and developing the idea was a journey filled with excitement and discovery, it was the final stretch, the implementation and commercialization, that posed the greatest challenge. This scenario is not unique to me; it's a common story in the world of innovation and entrepreneurship. We often find ourselves equipped with brilliant ideas and prototypes, yet the journey to bring these to fruition, to traverse that final 20%, becomes a more difficult path than we initially envisioned.

Common Roadblocks at 80%

Reaching the 80% mark in any project or venture is an achievement, but it's often beyond this point that some of the toughest roadblocks emerge. These obstacles, varied in nature, can significantly hinder the journey to completion.

One common roadblock is the shift from conceptual development to practical execution. For instance, a tech entrepreneur might find the initial stages of designing a software product exhilarating. The ideas flow, the design takes shape, and the potential seems limitless. However, as they move into the nitty-gritty of debugging, compliance, and user testing, the progress can feel frustratingly slow. This transition from a world of ideas to the realm of practicalities can be jarring and often leads to a sense of disillusionment.

Another typical roadblock is resource depletion. Consider an author writing their debut novel. The first few chapters are written with passion and fluidity, but as the story progresses toward its climax and conclusion, the writer may begin to feel drained – both creatively and physically. The resource here isn't just time or money; it's also the creative energy and enthusiasm that was plentiful at the start.

Similarly, in the world of startups, the initial fundraising and buzz creation can be exciting and rewarding. Yet, as the business shifts towards more operational and growth-focused activities—managing day-to-day operations, addressing customer service concerns, or scaling the product—the founders might find these tasks less invigorating, leading to a slowdown in momentum.

These specific examples resonate with the experiences of many who have found themselves bogged down in the final stages of their projects. Whether it's a creative endeavor, a technological innovation, or a business venture, the final 20% often introduces challenges that are markedly different from those encountered at the outset. Recognizing and understanding these roadblocks is the first step in developing strategies to navigate them successfully.

The Psychology Behind the Final 20%

As we approach the final stages of any project, the momentum that once drove us forward begins to wane. The initial surge of energy and optimism gives way to a more challenging phase, where progress slows, and each step feels more difficult. The early excitement fades as the work becomes more detailed and complex, and the finish line, though closer, can seem increasingly distant.

This shift occurs because the final stages of a project often demand a higher level of precision and greater attention to detail. The broad strokes that propelled us through the early phases are no longer sufficient; now, it's about refining, perfecting, and overcoming obstacles that were easier to overlook in the beginning. This is when every effort seems to yield less visible progress, leading to frustration and the temptation to give up.

It's important to recognize that this sense of slowing down is a natural part of the process. The closer we get to completing something, the more we tend to scrutinize our work, striving for excellence. This can make the final 20% feel like the hardest part, but it's also the most crucial. This stage challenges our perseverance and resilience, testing our commitment to see things through to the end.

When we reach this point, it's essential to remind ourselves that "the moment you feel like giving up is the moment you need to push harder. You're closer than you think." This mindset is essential in combating the mental and emotional fatigue that often sets in during this phase. Recognizing that this feeling of stagnation is temporary can be empowering. It's an indication that you're entering the final, crucial phase of your journey.

> ***"The moment you feel like giving up is the moment you need to push harder. You're closer than you think."***

The last 20% isn't just about completing the project; it's about finishing strong. It requires us to dig deep, find that extra reserve of energy, and push beyond the mental barriers that can hold us back. By maintaining our focus on the ultimate goal and understanding that the challenges we face are a natural part of the process, we can overcome this final hurdle and achieve the success we've worked so hard to reach.

Strategies for Overcoming Completion Hurdles

Overcoming the hurdles encountered in the final 20% of a project is both a challenge and an opportunity for growth. Remember, every hurdle, no matter how complex it may seem, is doable. The key lies in shifting our perspective and approach towards these obstacles.

It's essential to recognize that what we perceive as impossible hurdles are often opportunities in disguise. History is full of instances where tasks once deemed impossible were achieved. The four-minute mile, once considered beyond human capability, was eventually broken, setting a new standard for runners. In the realm of technology, the idea of sending humans to the moon was once a figment of science fiction, until it wasn't. These milestones remind us that the line between the impossible and the possible is often a matter of perception and persistence.

Drawing inspiration from past successes, both personally and from others, can be a powerful motivator. Reflect on times when you overcame challenges and remember the strategies and mindsets that helped you prevail. This reflection can reignite the belief in your ability to overcome current hurdles.

Remember, the final 20% might be tough, but it's also where true accomplishment lies. Embrace the challenges, not as barriers to your goal, but as essential parts of the journey that test and ultimately strengthen your resolve. No matter how large the hurdle may appear, with creativity, persistence, and a step-by-step approach, it can be overcome.

Maintaining Momentum

Maintaining momentum in the final stages of a project is less about speed and more about consistent forward movement. It's a common misconception that momentum equates to how fast we are moving towards our goal. In reality, momentum is about the persistence of motion, regardless of the pace.

Consider the analogy of running a marathon. The idea of running 26.2 miles in one go can be overwhelming. However, when you break it down to running 100 yards at a time, the task becomes more manageable. Each 100-yard stretch completed is an achievement, bringing you closer to the finish line. This approach can be applied to any project. Breaking down the overwhelming final 20% into smaller, achievable segments can transform a task that may seem unachievable into a series of manageable steps.

Just as a marathon runner conserves energy for the long haul, pacing yourself is crucial. It's about finding a rhythm that allows for steady progress while avoiding burnout. There will be moments of quick progress and times when you need to slow down. What's important is that you keep moving forward.

Remember, momentum is not just physical – it's also mental and emotional. Keeping your spirits up, staying motivated, and pushing forward, even when progress feels slow, are all integral to maintaining momentum. It's about the resilience to continue, the determination to keep going, and the belief that every small step is a vital part of the journey to completion.

Setting Realistic Milestones

In the pursuit of completing the final 20% of a project, the importance of setting realistic milestones cannot be overstated. Realistic milestones act as beacons on the path to completion, guiding and motivating us through the final stretch. The key is in setting goals that are ambitious enough to drive progress, yet attainable enough to avoid constant setbacks.

The challenge of setting realistic milestones lies in striking a balance between aspiration and practicality. Overly ambitious goals, while seemingly motivating, can lead to frustration and feelings of inadequacy when they are not met. On the other hand, milestones that are too easily achievable may not provide enough challenge to stimulate meaningful progress.

To set effective milestones, start by evaluating what is realistically achievable given your resources, time, and constraints. Consider breaking down the final phase of your project into smaller tasks and then estimate a reasonable time frame for each. This approach will assist in greater success and provide a clear path forward with achievable checkpoints along the way.

Each milestone reached is a victory, a testament to your persistence and effort. It's essential to take a moment to acknowledge and celebrate these achievements. Doing so reinforces a sense of success and builds confidence. These small celebrations act as fuel, propelling you forward and keeping the momentum alive. They serve as reminders of how far you've come and provide encouragement for the journey that remains.

Remember, the journey to completion is not just about reaching the end but also about the small victories along the way. Setting and achieving realistic milestones is a strategy that not only maintains momentum but also nurtures a continuous sense of accomplishment, keeping you motivated and focused as you navigate the final, most challenging part of your project.

Celebrating Progress

In the journey towards completing a project, especially in the challenging final 20%, celebrating progress, no matter how small, is crucial. It's easy to overlook the small victories when fixated on the end goal, but acknowledging these successes is vital in maintaining motivation and momentum.

Each step forward, every task completed, and each milestone reached is a marker of progress. These accomplishments, however insignificant they may seem in isolation, collectively represent the journey toward your goal. Celebrating these achievements serves multiple purposes. Firstly, it helps keep the initial thrill and excitement of the project alive. Remembering why you started and recognizing how far you've come rekindles that initial spark of enthusiasm.

Secondly, celebrating progress fosters a positive mindset. It shifts focus from what's left to be done to what has already been accomplished. This perspective is essential because it transforms the journey into a series of achievements rather than an endless grind. It's about shifting the narrative from 'I still have so much to do' to 'Look at all I've achieved.'

Moreover, these celebrations act as motivational milestones. They are reminders that you are capable, that you are moving forward, and that each step takes you closer to your ultimate goal. They provide an opportunity to pause, reflect, and recharge before tackling the next phase of your project.

Celebrating progress doesn't necessarily mean grand gestures. It can be as simple as taking a moment to acknowledge your hard work, sharing your achievements with friends, family, or colleagues, or treating yourself to a well-deserved break. The act of celebrating is less about the scale of the achievement and more about acknowledging and valuing your efforts.

Remember, progress, in any form, is a key component of success. By celebrating these small victories, you not only maintain a positive and productive mindset but also pave the way for future successes. It's these moments that make the journey worthwhile, keeping the flame of your initial vision and excitement burning bright as you navigate toward completion.

The Impact of Perfectionism

As we enter the final 20%, it is important to address the double-edged sword of perfectionism. While the pursuit of perfection can drive us to improve, it can also morph into a relentless quest for an unattainable ideal. Perfection, in many ways, is a flawed concept because it suggests a state that is beyond improvement, beyond human reach. Instead, what we should aim for in our endeavors is **greatness**.

Greatness is about doing your best, pushing your boundaries, and then being at peace with the outcome. It's a more compassionate and realistic goal, one that acknowledges our efforts and accepts our human limitations. Striving for greatness allows for growth, learning, and satisfaction, whereas chasing perfection can lead to endless cycles of revisions and dissatisfaction.

When we fixate on achieving perfection, we set ourselves up for a journey with no real destination. Perfection is subjective and often an ever-shifting target. This endless pursuit can extend our efforts indefinitely, leaving projects perpetually unfinished or never quite good enough by our own standards. It's vital to recognize when it's time to step back and appreciate the work we've done.

Hard work, dedication, and a commitment to doing your best are commendable qualities. Learning to be content with the result, not because it's perfect, but because it represents your greatest effort, is a skill worth cultivating. This mindset doesn't mean settling for average results; instead, it means acknowledging and appreciating the moment when your hard work and the outcome come together to create something truly meaningful.

As we strive to navigate through the final stages of our projects, let's shift our focus from the unattainable ideal of perfection to the achievable reality of greatness. This approach will not only lead to more completed projects but also to a greater sense of fulfillment and accomplishment.

Chapter 3:
Ideas Without Action

In the vast expanse of human creativity, every idea holds potential value, like seeds waiting to be nurtured into life. Often, we are struck by sudden flashes of inspiration – ideas that surge within us, brimming with the possibility of innovation and change. Yet, all too frequently, these sparks of creativity are allowed to fade away, extinguished before they even have a chance to ignite fully.

It's crucial to recognize the inherent worth in each idea that crosses our minds. We are often quick to judge our own thoughts, dismissing them as impractical or unachievable without giving them the opportunity to be explored. However, the truth is, we never know which idea might hold the potential to make a real impact. History is filled with stories of simple concepts that transformed into world-changing realities.

Embracing our ideas, regardless of how unformed or unconventional they may seem, is the first step in a journey of potential discovery and innovation. This initial phase of acknowledging and valuing our ideas is critical. It's about allowing ourselves to dream, to wonder, and to imagine the possibilities that each new thought brings. It's in this phase that we lay the foundation for what could become a life-changing project, a groundbreaking invention, or a new artistic endeavor.

So, as we navigate through this expanse, let's remind ourselves to give our ideas the attention they deserve. Each one holds a universe of potential, and it is up to us to explore and nurture these seeds of creativity. The next big breakthrough could be residing in your next thought, waiting for the chance to be brought to life.

The Transition from Thought to Action

Every groundbreaking invention and every monumental discovery in history began as a single thought in someone's mind. This transition from a fleeting idea to a tangible action is what differentiates a dream that fades away from one that changes the course of history.

Consider the light bulb, an invention that revolutionized the way we live. It started as a thought in Thomas Edison's mind. Imagine if Edison had never acted on his idea if he had let it remain just a passing thought. The world might have lingered in gaslight longer, delaying progress in countless fields.

Or take the Wright brothers, whose curiosity and determination led them to question the possibility of flight. Their journey from mere thought to the first successful airplane flight transformed the world, making global travel a reality. If they had not pursued their idea with action, the entire trajectory of global connectivity and travel might have been different.

In the realm of technology, consider the impact of personal computers. Visionaries like Steve Jobs and Bill Gates had the foresight to see the potential of computers in every home. Their initial ideas could have easily been dismissed as unrealistic or too ambitious. Yet, their decision to act on these thoughts fundamentally altered the fabric of modern society, from how we work to how we communicate.

These examples underscore a crucial reality: the transition from thought to action is a decisive moment. If the initial idea for the light bulb, the airplane, or the personal computer had not been pursued with deliberate action, our world might look entirely different today. The potential loss of progress highlights the significance of not just having ideas but acting on them.

Thus, as we consider our own ideas, it's essential to remember that the journey of a thousand miles begins with a single step. Every great invention, every innovation, and every leap forward started with someone deciding to take that first step. It's a compelling call to not just dream but to do, to not just imagine but to implement.

Common Pitfalls in Executing Ideas

Transforming an idea into action is often weighed down with hurdles, each presenting its unique challenge. Anticipating these challenges and being prepared to navigate them is crucial in the journey from conception to realization. Let's explore some common pitfalls and strategies for overcoming them.

One significant challenge is resource limitation. For instance, an entrepreneur might have an innovative business idea but lacks the necessary funding or technical expertise to bring it to life. Overcoming this requires creativity and resourcefulness. Crowdfunding, networking to find the right partners, or upskilling oneself are ways to bridge this gap. It's about finding alternative paths and leveraging available resources to their fullest potential.

Another obstacle often encountered is resistance to change, either from within or from external stakeholders. Imagine an employee in a large corporation proposing a radical new process. The challenge here isn't just in the idea's execution but also in convincing others of its merit. Overcoming this resistance involves building a convincing case, showcasing potential benefits, and gaining small wins to demonstrate the idea's value.

Market dynamics and consumer behavior present another layer of complexity. A product designer might conceive an innovative product, only to find that market trends shift, or consumer preferences change. Staying adaptable, conducting continuous market research, and being willing to pivot are key strategies to navigate this challenge.

In facing these challenges, the key lies in resilience and adaptability. Challenges should be seen as opportunities rather than roadblocks. Each one overcome brings you closer to your goal and often provides valuable lessons that refine and improve your original idea.

The Graveyard of Dreams

The 'graveyard of dreams' doesn't just house our unrealized dreams; it also stands as a heartbreaking reminder of what could have been. Reflecting on my own experience with the final project in my Computer Information Systems program, I realize now how it represented not just a missed opportunity but a tangible possibility that was within reach.

That project, a POS application interfacing with a PDA for restaurant orders, was more than just an academic exercise. It was a feasible, forward-thinking idea with the potential to change the industry – and it eventually did, though not through my efforts. Thus, it became a part of this silent graveyard, not because it lacked viability, but because I didn't take the next steps to bring it to fruition.

Looking back, I recognize that it wasn't just about the technical feasibility of the idea. It was about the belief in its potential and the courage to take it beyond the confines of a classroom. The realization that this idea was indeed possible, yet remained unexplored, brings both regret and enlightenment.

However, rather than dwelling on what was lost, such experiences can serve as powerful catalysts for future action. They remind us that our ideas do have potential and that the gap between possibility and realization is often not as wide as it seems. These experiences in the graveyard of dreams are not just monuments to past failures but are fuel for future endeavors.

Let these silent monuments in your own graveyard of dreams be a source of motivation. Let them remind you that every idea you have is a seed of possibility, deserving of consideration and action. As we move forward, we must use these past experiences not as anchors of regret but as springboards that propel us into action. The next idea you have could be the one that not only escapes the graveyard but flourishes in the world of realized dreams.

Overcoming Inertia

Overcoming the inertia that often hinders the early stages of executing an idea is vital to turning vibrant concepts into reality rather than letting them fade away. Inertia, in this context, refers to the resistance to change or the difficulty in starting new tasks due to comfort with the current state or lack of motivation. A useful way to combat this stagnation is by simplifying the process. Rather than tackling everything at once, start with the most approachable aspects of your goal. This strategy allows you to gradually build momentum, making the larger objective seem less daunting and more achievable.

Integrating work on your project into your daily or weekly routine is crucial for maintaining consistency. Even dedicating a small, regular amount of time can lead to significant progress over time, helping to overcome the paralysis of inaction and keeping your idea at the forefront of your priorities. Techniques like the Pomodoro Technique, which involves working in focused intervals (typically 25 minutes) followed by short breaks (usually 5 minutes), can increase productivity and prevent burnout. This method helps to maintain concentration and momentum, making it easier to start and continue working on your project.

Leveraging accountability by sharing your goals with a mentor, peer, or support group can also be a powerful motivator. Knowing that someone else is aware of your goals and progress can spur you on. Additionally, recognizing and celebrating each small achievement can boost morale and provide the energy needed to continue. This recognition transforms the journey into a series of successes rather than a long haul towards a distant goal.

By focusing on these strategies, the task of bringing an idea to life becomes a series of practical and manageable steps. This methodical approach can significantly impact advancing an idea more effectively than trying to tackle everything at once. Consistently taking small actions leads to substantial progress, transforming how ideas are realized and ensuring they come to fruition.

Case Studies of Lost Opportunities

The landscape of history and personal growth is often marked by 'what ifs' – opportunities missed due to inaction or hesitation. Examining these cases offers valuable lessons on the importance of seizing opportunities when they arise.

In the business world, a classic example is that of Xerox in the 1970s. Xerox's Palo Alto Research Center (PARC) was at the forefront of developing the technology that would later become the foundation of personal computing – including the graphical user interface (GUI), the mouse, and Ethernet. These groundbreaking innovations had the potential to transform the tech industry. However, Xerox failed to capitalize on these technologies, focusing instead on their core business of copiers. Meanwhile, companies like Apple and Microsoft recognized the immense potential of these innovations. Apple, in particular, incorporated the GUI and mouse into its Macintosh computers, revolutionizing personal computing. This inaction resulted in Xerox missing out on dominating the promising personal computing industry, and their innovations were left to benefit others.

Similarly, Kodak's hesitation to embrace digital photography – a technology they themselves invented – is another example of a missed opportunity with far-reaching consequences. Kodak was a pioneer in the photography industry, but their leadership feared that digital photography would cannibalize their highly profitable film business. Despite having the first digital camera prototype in 1975, Kodak delayed its development and marketing. As competitors like Sony and Canon advanced in the digital arena, Kodak struggled to catch up. By the time Kodak fully committed to digital, they had lost their market leadership and faced severe financial difficulties. This reluctance to innovate ultimately led to Kodak filing for bankruptcy in 2012, a sharp departure from its former dominance.

Another notable case is that of Blockbuster. At its peak, Blockbuster was a giant in the video rental industry with thousands of stores worldwide. However, in the early 2000s, when Netflix approached Blockbuster with an offer to sell their company for $50 million, Blockbuster's leadership dismissed the idea, failing to recognize the potential of online streaming. Netflix continued to innovate, shifting from DVD rentals by mail to a streaming service that revolutionized the entertainment industry. Blockbuster, on the other hand, clung to its traditional business model and struggled to adapt to the digital age. This reluctance to innovate and adapt to changing consumer behaviors led to Blockbuster's eventual bankruptcy in 2010, leaving Netflix to dominate the market they could have co-owned.

These case studies underscore a crucial lesson: inaction and hesitation can lead to significant missed opportunities. They highlight the importance of embracing chances when they come, even if they push us out of our comfort zones. It's not just about the opportunities we seize but also about the lessons we learn and the growth we experience when we choose action over inaction.

Developing a Bias for Action

Developing an action-oriented mindset is essential for transforming ideas into tangible results, marking a significant shift from excessive contemplation to proactive engagement. To cultivate such a mindset, start by setting clear, specific goals that prompt immediate action. For example, rather than a vague aim like "work on my project," specify what "working" entails, such as "complete the first draft of the business plan by next Friday." This clarity in goal setting is the first step toward actionable progress.

If procrastination becomes a barrier, the '5-minute rule' can be a powerful tool. By committing to work on a task for just five minutes, the initial inertia often gives way to a more sustained effort. This approach tackles the challenge of starting, which is frequently the hardest part. Along with this, cutting down on planning time can help avoid the paralysis that often comes from overthinking. By setting a strict limit on planning duration, the focus shifts towards execution once the planning phase is complete.

Adopting a 'Do it Now' philosophy for tasks that take a few minutes or less helps build a consistent sense of achievement and prevents the accumulation of minor tasks. Visualizing the end result of your efforts can also keep you motivated, focusing your energy on the satisfaction of achieving your goals. To further enhance productivity, limiting decision fatigue by planning your schedule in advance or establishing set routines ensures that your mental energy is reserved for significant tasks.

Regular reflection on the cost of inaction, such as considering the missed opportunities that arise from stagnation, can serve as a potent motivator. Seeking constructive feedback from trusted individuals can provide new perspectives and motivation, enhancing the quality of your work. Celebrating even the smallest step toward your goals reinforces positive behavior and encourages ongoing action.

Finally, staying accountable by sharing your action plans with someone who can hold you accountable ensures that you have the external push needed to remain committed to your goals. By integrating these strategies into your daily routine, you transition from a state of contemplation to one of action, significantly boosting your chances of success. This methodical approach to implementing ideas not only increases your project completion rate but also turns your dreams into achievable realities, marking a crucial shift towards becoming action-driven.

The Role of Accountability

Accountability, both from ourselves and from others, plays a key role in translating ideas into action. It serves as a powerful catalyst, pushing us beyond mere intention into the realm of tangible progress.

Holding ourselves accountable is about owning our actions and decisions. It's acknowledging that the responsibility to act on our ideas rests primarily with us. This form of self-accountability acts as an internal compass, guiding our daily decisions and actions in alignment with our goals. It involves setting personal standards and expectations, and then honestly evaluating our progress against them.

However, self-accountability has its limits. Our internal biases can lead to justifications or excuses for inaction. This is where external accountability becomes vital. Incorporating friends, family, mentors, or peers into our accountability framework can significantly enhance our ability to act. These individuals can provide the external perspective and motivation necessary to push us forward. They act as sounding boards, offering honest feedback, encouragement, and sometimes the tough love needed to keep us on track.

For instance, sharing your goal to launch a new business with a trusted mentor not only commits you to the idea but also opens avenues for support and guidance. Regular check-ins with this mentor can keep you accountable, ensuring that you're making consistent progress.

Similarly, joining a peer group with similar goals or challenges can provide a shared accountability structure. In such groups, members hold each other accountable, celebrate successes, and provide support during setbacks. This collective journey fosters a sense of commitment and can be incredibly motivating.

Accountability, especially when shared, can transform the way we approach our goals. Knowing that someone else is aware of our objectives and is expecting us to follow through can be a powerful motivator. It adds a layer of responsibility and urgency that self-accountability alone may not provide.

Moreover, accountability partners can help us break through moments of doubt or inertia. They can remind us of our capabilities and our reasons for pursuing our goals in the first place. This external push can often be the difference between remaining stuck and moving forward.

While self-accountability is crucial, external accountability can be the additional driving force needed to turn ideas into actions. It's about harnessing the power of our relationships to fuel our journey toward success, making the process of achieving our goals not just a personal endeavor, but a shared one.

Reflecting on Unfulfilled Ideas

Looking back at our unfulfilled ideas and projects can often suggest a sense of failure. It's natural to feel a tinge of regret or disappointment when thinking about what could have been. However, dwelling on these feelings can create a self-fulfilling prophecy of failure, shaping our mindset to anticipate defeat in future endeavors. It's crucial, therefore, to shift our perspective on these past experiences.

Instead of viewing unfulfilled ideas as failures, we can choose to see them as valuable lessons. This shift in mindset from "I failed" to "How can I do this better next time?" is transformative. It encourages a constructive analysis of past endeavors, turning each unfulfilled idea into a building block for future success.

> ***"How can I do this better next time?"***

One effective way to learn from unfulfilled ideas is to pinpoint the distinct moment where excitement turned into overwhelm. Was it a lack of resources, a fear of the unknown, or perhaps a shift in priorities? By identifying this turning point, you can gain insights into what derailed your progress. Understanding these triggers helps in developing strategies to avoid similar pitfalls in the future.

Reflect on each unfulfilled idea and dissect what went wrong. Was it the execution, the planning, or external factors beyond your control? Analyzing these aspects can reveal patterns and areas for improvement. Perhaps you needed more research, better planning, or a different approach to problem-solving.

Also, consider what you did well. Recognizing your strengths even in unfulfilled projects can bolster your confidence and provide a solid foundation for your next venture.

Use these reflections constructively. Each lesson learned from an unfulfilled idea is a tool in your arsenal for future projects. If resource management was an issue, consider how you can better allocate resources next time. If fear holds you back, explore ways to build confidence or reduce risks.

    Remember, every successful person has a history of unfulfilled ideas. What sets them apart is their ability to learn from these experiences and apply these lessons moving forward. Embracing this approach transforms your history of unfulfilled ideas from a narrative of failure to a roadmap of resilience and growth.

Chapter 4: Silencing the Fear Within

Fear, in its essence, is an emotional response triggered by perceived threats, which can be physical, emotional, or psychological. It is a fundamental, deeply wired reaction, essential for survival, prompting the fight-or-flight response in dangerous situations. However, in the modern context, fear often transcends physical threats and manifests in areas that challenge our comfort, aspirations, and identity.

This primal response can influence us profoundly in all life areas, not just in pursuing dreams, ideas, or business ventures. Fear can shape our relationships, career choices, personal growth, and even day-to-day decisions. It operates on various levels – from the fear of making a wrong decision in daily life to deeper fears that impact our life trajectories.

For instance, fear can manifest as hesitation in voicing an opinion, reluctance to take on new challenges at work, or avoidance of social situations. It can be as subtle as the unease in trying new experiences or as significant as the dread of taking major life steps like changing careers or relocating.

Understanding fear involves recognizing its different forms and the common thread they share – the anticipation of negative outcomes. Whether it's fear of failure, judgment, or the unknown, at its core, fear often revolves around the worry of not meeting expectations, whether our own or those perceived from others.

Acknowledging that fear is a natural and universal experience is the first step in addressing its impact. By understanding that fear's role extends beyond life's big decisions to everyday situations, we can begin to see how it shapes our behavior and choices. This awareness is crucial in developing strategies to manage fear, ensuring it doesn't become a barrier to action and fulfillment in various life aspects.

Fear of Failure

The fear of failure is a deeply ingrained emotion that often finds its roots early in our lives. It can originate from various sources – parental expectations, academic pressures, early experiences of disappointment, or societal norms that equate success with self-worth. These early influences can profoundly shape our perception of failure, turning it into something to be avoided at all costs.

As children and adolescents, experiences of falling short – whether in academics, sports, or social settings – can leave lasting imprints. A failed test, a lost game, or a rejected social advance can significantly impact a young mind. When these experiences are met with criticism rather than support and understanding, the fear of failing becomes embedded in our psyche. It starts to dictate how we approach challenges and opportunities, leading to avoidance of situations where there's a risk of failing.

As we carry this fear into adulthood, it continues to influence our decisions and actions. It manifests in our reluctance to pursue new ventures or career paths, our hesitation to express ourselves creatively, or our tendency to stay in safe, familiar environments. The fear of failing, once rooted, can create a pattern of behavior where playing it safe becomes the norm.

This fear is often compounded by the pervasive notion in society that failure is inherently negative – a notion that overlooks the value of failure as a learning and growth opportunity. The narrative around failure needs a shift – from seeing it as a mark of defeat to viewing it as an integral part of the learning process.

To break free from the paralyzing grip of the fear of failure, we must first acknowledge its origins and understand how it has shaped our mindset over the years. Reflecting on our past – the moments we've perceived as failures – and reassessing them can be enlightening. It's about recognizing that every so-called failure is an opportunity for learning and growth.

Facing the fear of failure involves a conscious effort to challenge and reframe our perception of what it means to fail. It requires building a mindset that embraces risks, understands the value of mistakes, and sees failure as a guidepost, not an endpoint.

Fear of Success

Surprisingly, for many of us, the fear that lurks in the shadows of our aspirations is not the fear of failure, but the fear of success. It's a paradoxical situation where the very outcome we strive for becomes a source of anxiety. This fear often goes unrecognized because, on the surface, who wouldn't want to succeed? Yet, beneath this surface lies a complex web of concerns about the implications of success.

One underlying cause of the fear of success is the change it brings. Success often means entering uncharted territory. It could mean new responsibilities, higher expectations, and more visibility. For some, this brings the fear of not being able to handle the new challenges or the pressure that comes with success. There's a comfort in the familiarity of current circumstances, even if they're limiting.

Another aspect is the fear of altered relationships. Success can change the dynamics in personal and professional relationships. There's a concern about becoming alienated from peers, friends, or even family members. People fear that success might make them appear different, arrogant, or unrelatable to their current social circle.

Additionally, there's the impostor syndrome – the feeling of not being worthy of success or the fear of being exposed as a fraud. Even when we've put in the effort and earned the recognition, a persistent voice questions our capabilities and accomplishments.

The fear of success can also stem from internalized beliefs and past experiences. If success was frowned upon, seen as a source of problems, or if early achievements led to negative experiences, this could create a subconscious aversion to success.

To overcome the fear of success, it's essential to confront these underlying issues. It involves recognizing that success is a natural progression of effort and talent, understanding that change is a part of growth, and learning to manage new challenges. It's also about redefining success on your own terms – aligning it with your values and what makes you genuinely fulfilled, rather than external perceptions of success.

Navigating the fear of success requires a balanced view of what achieving your goals will realistically entail. It's about preparing for the changes while staying true to your roots and values. Acknowledging and addressing these fears is the first step towards embracing success fully and without reservation.

Fear of Judgment

The fear of judgment is a powerful force that can significantly alter our course of action. It stems from a deep-seated human need for social acceptance and the fear of rejection, rooted in our evolutionary past. In our earliest communities, being excluded from the group could mean losing vital resources, protection, and ultimately, survival itself. While the stakes today are different, the underlying psychology remains just as strong.

In almost every endeavor, there is the potential for judgment. Whether it's starting a new business, changing career paths, or simply pursuing goals that differ from what others expect, the possibility of being judged by others is ever-present. This fear can become paralyzing, leading us to make choices that are more about pleasing others than pursuing what we have been called to do.

Sometimes, the judgment we fear is rooted in others' insecurities or their perspectives on what constitutes success and happiness. In some cases, it may even stem from their own fears or jealousy about our potential success. This can manifest as discouragement or negative feedback, aimed more at keeping us within familiar bounds rather than seeing us venture into new, potentially successful territories.

It's essential to remember that our life's journey is our own. The choices we make and the paths we pursue should be for ourselves, our fulfillment, and the well-being of our loved ones. What we are called to do – our passions and dreams – should be the driving force behind our actions, not the fear of others' opinions or judgments.

Overcoming the fear of judgment involves building self-confidence and self-esteem. It's about valuing our own opinions and decisions above others' unsolicited judgments. Cultivating a strong sense of self and focusing on personal goals can help diminish the weight of external opinions.

It's also important to surround ourselves with supportive and like-minded individuals who understand and encourage our aspirations. Having a network of people who believe in us can bolster our courage to take risks and make decisions that align with our true selves, regardless of external judgments.

In essence, navigating the fear of judgment is about prioritizing our happiness and fulfillment over societal expectations and opinions. It's a journey towards embracing our authenticity and living a life true to ourselves.

Fear of the Unknown

The fear of the unknown is a powerful barrier that often hinders exploration, innovation, and personal growth. It is rooted in our basic human instinct to seek safety and predictability. However, this fear can limit our potential to reach new heights, explore uncharted territories, and realize our most ambitious dreams.

The unknown represents a realm of endless possibilities, but it also holds uncertainties that can evoke anxiety. This fear can manifest in various forms – hesitation to change careers, reluctance to try new approaches, or procrastination in making significant life decisions. It is the uncertainty of outcomes that keeps us tethered to the familiar, often at the expense of our growth and fulfillment.

My journey to starting my own software company serves as a testament to the paralyzing effect of the fear of the unknown. For years, the idea lingered in my mind, but it was the uncertainty of stepping into uncharted waters that held me back. Questions like "What if it fails?" or "What if I'm not prepared?" dominated my thoughts, overshadowing the excitement and potential of my venture.

It was only when I confronted these fears, acknowledging that the unknown was a natural part of the journey, that things began to change. I realized that every successful venture begins with a leap of faith into the unknown. Embracing this uncertainty rather than fearing it became a turning point.

Once I let go of my fear and took that first definitive step, things started falling into place. It wasn't an immediate transformation, but a gradual process where each step forward revealed new opportunities and learnings. This experience taught me that the unknown, while scary at times, is often where the magic happens. It's where ideas take shape, potential is realized, and new paths are forged.

To overcome the fear of the unknown, one must adopt a mindset of exploration and curiosity. It's about viewing the unknown not as a threat, but as a space rich with potential. Embracing risk, being open to new experiences, and accepting that not knowing everything is not only okay but a part of the adventure, are crucial.

The unknown is an integral part of innovation. It is in this space that creativity flourishes and new ideas are born. By stepping into the unknown, we open ourselves to new possibilities and discoveries that can drive both personal and professional growth.

Confronting the fear of the unknown involves a shift in perspective – from viewing it as a barrier to seeing it as a gateway to new opportunities. It's about taking that leap of faith, knowing that while the path may not be clear, it is loaded with possibilities waiting to be discovered. It's okay to be scared, just don't let that fear stop you from doing what you were meant to achieve.

Building Resilience Against Fear

The influence of fear in our lives is determined largely by the power we choose to give it. It's an emotion rooted in our deepest instincts, originally designed as a mechanism of survival. Yet, in our modern lives, it often transcends physical threats, manifesting in our aspirations, relationships, and self-perception. Building resilience against fear isn't about eliminating it but about developing the mental and emotional strength to acknowledge fear without being overcome by it.

Understanding the nature of fear is essential. Recognizing that it is a common and natural response is the first step in mitigating its control over our decisions and actions. Fear is neutral – it is our reaction to it that shapes our experiences. By reframing how we perceive and react to fear, we start to strip away its overwhelming power.

Developing mental fortitude is a process of training the mind to approach fear with a balanced perspective. It involves recognizing the signals fear sends without letting it dictate our actions. Practices like mindfulness meditation, cognitive-behavioral techniques, and positive self-talk are instrumental in this regard. They help in reshaping our internal narrative, transforming the way we interpret and respond to fearful situations.

Equally important is emotional resilience – the ability to navigate through the feelings that fear evokes. This resilience can be fostered by acknowledging and expressing our fears in constructive ways, such as through journaling, art, or conversation. It's about creating a space where fear can be examined without judgment, allowing us to understand its roots and the messages it conveys.

Building resilience also means learning to distinguish between fears that are protective and those that are inhibitive. Not all fear is detrimental; some of it can act as a guide or a motivator, prompting caution or deeper reflection. The skill lies in discerning which fears to heed and which to challenge.

At its core, building resilience against fear is about empowerment. It's about developing the internal resources to face fear with composure and clarity, understanding that on the other side of fear often lies growth, learning, and opportunity. By cultivating this resilience, we can navigate through life's uncertainties with a sense of confidence and agency, transforming our relationship with fear from one of avoidance to one of understanding and mastery.

Overcoming Different Fears

J.K. Rowling's story is a powerful testament to overcoming the fear of failure. Before the success of the "Harry Potter" series, Rowling faced significant hardships. She was a single mother living on welfare, enduring numerous rejections from publishers. Yet, she persisted, driven by her passion for storytelling. Her resilience in the face of potential failure led to the creation of one of the most beloved book series in history, changing her life and the landscape of children's literature.

Howard Schultz, the mind behind Starbucks' transformation into a global brand, faced the fear of success when he proposed the idea of a coffee shop that would become a third place between work and home. Schultz's vision involved significant changes and risks that could alter his life and career dramatically. Embracing these changes, he moved forward, turning Starbucks into a household name and redefining coffee culture worldwide.

Oprah Winfrey's rise to becoming a media mogul was marked by overcoming the fear of judgment. Coming from a background of poverty and abuse, Winfrey faced societal judgments and stereotypes. Her determination to be authentic and speak her truth, especially on sensitive and personal topics, was initially met with skepticism. However, her authenticity resonated with millions, leading to the success of "The Oprah Winfrey Show" and her subsequent ventures.

Elon Musk's career is a series of ventures into the unknown, from PayPal to SpaceX and Tesla. Musk consistently stepped into uncharted territories, investing in industries where success was uncertain. His willingness to embrace the unknown and his vision for innovative technologies have made him a prominent figure in changing how we think about space travel, automotive transport, and sustainable energy.

These stories exemplify those fears of failure, success, judgment, and the unknown, while universal, can be conquered. Each of these individuals faced their fears head-on, using them as catalysts to drive their passion, creativity, and determination. Their triumphs remind us that on the other side of fear lies the potential for extraordinary achievement.

Leveraging Fear as a Growth Tool

The natural inclination when confronted with fear is often to retreat or avoid the source of that fear. However, embracing a different perspective can transform fear from a hindrance into a powerful tool for personal growth and success. This shift in mindset is about recognizing that the presence of fear, particularly in pursuits that cannot physically harm us, often signals that we are on the brink of something significant – a breakthrough, a learning opportunity, or a path to success.

When we encounter something that stirs fear within us, it's frequently because it pushes us out of our comfort zones. Whether it's the prospect of a new job, public speaking, or starting a business, these challenges provoke fear because they involve uncertainty and potential for change. However, it's precisely these scenarios that provide the richest opportunities for growth. The unease we feel can be a sign that we are on the verge of developing new skills, gaining new insights, or achieving something we once thought impossible.

The key to leveraging fear is in reframing. Instead of viewing fear as a stop sign, we can choose to see it as a marker on the path to personal development. This perspective involves acknowledging fear but not allowing it to dictate our decisions. It's about saying, "Yes, this scares me, but that fear is not a reason to stop. It's a reason to proceed with caution, preparedness, and an open mind."

> *"Yes, this scares me, but that fear is not a reason to stop. It's a reason to proceed with caution, preparedness, and an open mind."*

Often, our greatest potential lies just beyond what scares us. By pushing through fear, we uncover abilities and strengths we didn't know we had. This process can be immensely rewarding, not just in terms of achieving external goals but also in building self-confidence and resilience.

Fear can also act as a motivator. The adrenaline rush, the heightened senses that come with fear, can be channeled into focused action. This harnessing of fear's energy can propel us forward, fueling our efforts and sharpening our focus on the task at hand.

Leveraging fear as a tool for growth involves a conscious choice to face what scares us, to extract lessons from these experiences, and to use these insights to propel ourselves forward. It's about recognizing that on the other side of fear lies the realization of our dreams and goals, and that the journey through fear is a valuable part of our personal and professional development.

A Supportive Environment for Facing Fears

As we navigate through the challenges posed by various fears, the role of a supportive environment cannot be overstated. While it's possible to confront and overcome fears independently, the journey is often more fruitful with a support network. This support can come in various forms – family, friends, mentors, professional counselors, or peer groups – each playing a crucial role in alleviating the intensity of our fears and paving the way for progress.

Knowing you're not alone in your fears can be incredibly reassuring. A supportive network provides a sense of solidarity and understanding. Sharing experiences with others who have faced similar fears can offer new perspectives, strategies for coping, and, most importantly, the realization that your fears are not unique to you. This shared experience can demystify fears and make them more manageable.

In moments when fear feels overwhelming, having someone to turn to for emotional support can make a significant difference. A supportive friend, family member, or mentor can offer encouragement, reassurance, and a listening ear. They can remind you of your strengths and achievements, helping to boost your confidence and resolve.

A supportive network can provide diverse viewpoints and advice. This can be particularly beneficial when fear clouds judgment. Others can offer objective insights, help brainstorm solutions, and provide constructive feedback that might not be apparent from a singular perspective.

A support system can also serve as a source of accountability. Sharing your goals and the fears you're trying to overcome with others can motivate you to act. Knowing that others are aware of your objectives and are rooting for you can be a powerful motivator to push through fear and work towards your goals.

In some cases, especially when fears are deeply rooted or overwhelming, seeking support from a professional therapist or counselor can be beneficial. They can offer specialized techniques and guidance tailored to your specific fears, providing a structured approach to overcoming them.

Whether it's the comfort of shared experiences, the boost from emotional support, the clarity from diverse perspectives, the drive from accountability, or the guidance from professional support, a network of encouragement and understanding can be a vital asset in transforming fear from a barrier to a catalyst for growth.

Chapter 5: The Landscape of Limitations

At the outset of this exploration into the landscape of limitations, it's crucial first to understand what we mean by 'limitations.' In its broadest sense, a limitation is anything that constrains us or holds us back from achieving our full potential. These can be external barriers, such as societal norms, physical constraints, or resource limitations, or they can be internal, such as mental blocks, ingrained beliefs, or emotional hurdles.

Limitations manifest in various ways across the spectrum of our lives. In our professional lives, they can appear as ceilings we hit in our careers, perhaps due to a lack of resources, opportunities, or other external challenges. In personal development, limitations might take the form of ingrained beliefs about our capabilities, often influenced by our upbringing, culture, or past experiences. Even in our relationships, limitations can emerge, restricting how we connect and interact with others, often shaped by past hurts or a lack of emotional intelligence.

It's important to note that limitations are not inherently negative. They often serve as a natural boundary of our current state of being or understanding. However, when these limitations prevent us from reaching our goals, fulfilling our potential, or living our lives to the fullest, they become barriers that must be addressed.

Understanding limitations requires a well-rounded approach. It involves self-reflection to recognize our internal barriers, awareness to identify external constraints, and the willingness to confront these limitations honestly. This part of our journey aims to guide you through this process – to help you identify, understand, and eventually navigate the landscape of your own limitations.

As we dive deeper, we will explore not just the nature of these limitations but also how they mold our lives, often without our conscious realization. By bringing these limitations into the light, we equip ourselves with the power to challenge and overcome them, paving the way for growth, success, and a fuller realization of our potential.

Self-Imposed vs. External Limitations

Understanding the distinction between self-imposed and external limitations is a critical step in navigating the landscape of our personal and professional lives. This understanding helps us identify the source of our constraints and, as a result, the appropriate strategies to overcome them.

Self-imposed limitations are the barriers that we create for ourselves. They often stem from our beliefs, fears, and attitudes toward our abilities and potential. For example, a person might believe they are not intelligent enough to pursue a certain career, or they may fear that trying something new will lead to failure. These internal dialogues and beliefs limit our actions and can keep us from attempting to achieve our goals. They are often rooted in past experiences, negative self-talk, or the internalization of critical judgments from others.

External limitations are imposed by factors outside our immediate control. They can include socio-economic constraints, physical or geographical barriers, societal norms, or even the state of the economy. For instance, an individual with a great business idea might be limited by a lack of capital, or someone living in a remote area may have limited access to educational resources. These external factors are often more tangible than self-imposed limitations, but they can be just as constraining.

Recognizing the difference between these two types of limitations is essential because it influences how we address them. Overcoming self-imposed limitations often requires internal work – changing our mindset, challenging our belief systems, and developing greater self-awareness. Overcoming external limitations, on the other hand, might involve seeking external resources, advocating for change, or finding creative ways to work within or around these constraints.

For example, consider someone who aspires to be a professional artist. A self-imposed limitation might be their belief that they aren't talented enough. To overcome this, they would need to work on building confidence and reframe their self-perception. In contrast, an external limitation could be the lack of a local market for their art. Overcoming this might involve exploring online platforms or relocating to a more art-friendly community.

Understanding these differences allows us to target our efforts and resources more effectively in overcoming the limitations that stand in our way. It empowers us to take specific, targeted actions based on the nature of the barriers we face.

The Impact of Limitations on Growth

Limitations, especially those we impose upon ourselves, can have a significant impact on our ability to grow, innovate, and achieve our dreams. They often act as invisible barriers, holding us back from realizing our full potential. My personal journey in starting my own business is a testament to this truth.

For 13 years, I grappled with self-imposed limitations. Despite having a vision and a passion for launching a software company, I continually doubted my capabilities, particularly my business intelligence. The fear of failure loomed large, casting a shadow over my aspirations. This fear, coupled with my perceived lack of knowledge, became a formidable barrier, delaying the launch of my business. It was a clear illustration of how our internal limitations can stall our progress, sometimes for years.

Reflecting on this phase of my life, I often remind myself of an important truth: "The only limits in life are the ones we set ourselves." We often create boundaries in our minds that

> **"The only limits in life are the ones we set ourselves."**

are far more restrictive than any external factors. These mental barriers are rooted in fear, doubt, and sometimes a lack of self-belief. They shape our decisions, our actions, and, ultimately, the trajectory of our lives.

The impact of these limitations is not just about missed opportunities or delayed ventures. It's about the personal growth that we forfeit when we allow our fears and doubts to dictate our choices. Every time we surrender to these internal barriers, we lose a chance to learn, to evolve, and to expand our horizons.

Breaking free from these self-imposed limitations is essential for personal and professional development. It involves a shift in mindset, a conscious effort to challenge our fears, and an understanding that growth often lies just beyond the boundaries we create for ourselves. In launching my business eventually, I had to confront these fears and move past them. It was a journey of not only building a business but also of personal transformation.

By exploring these invisible barriers in more depth, understanding their origins, and most importantly, uncovering strategies to overcome them, we empower ourselves to pursue our goals with a renewed sense of confidence and limitless potential.

Identifying Our Limitations

Understanding the scope of our limitations, both those readily apparent and those lurking beneath the surface, requires a shift in perspective, often looking from the outside in. One effective approach is objective self-observation, where we step back and view our actions and decisions as if we were an outsider. This detached viewpoint, like giving advice to a friend, can reveal patterns and choices that suggest self-imposed limitations.

Another powerful tool in uncovering these hidden barriers is external feedback. We are often too close to our situation to see it clearly. Regular and honest feedback from colleagues, mentors, or friends can illuminate areas where we might unknowingly be holding ourselves back or where external factors are restricting our progress. Engaging in role reversal exercises further enhances this perspective shift. By adopting the viewpoint of someone observing us, such as a boss or a peer, we can gain insights into limitations that might otherwise remain unnoticed.

For example, a good friend of mine and I were talking one day, and she mentioned how she started writing a song, and had gotten far in the lyrics, but then she just stopped and hadn't worked on it in over a year. She mentioned how she would love to finish it someday. My response to her was, "Well what's holding you back?" She looked at me with a blank stare for a moment and responded with, "You know what, nothing is holding me back." This simple realization helped re-spark that excitement she once had. She went on to finish writing the song, recorded a demo, and even had a music video made. I didn't give her any great advice; she just needed someone to hold her accountable. Having that external accountability can sometimes be the one thing we need to remove the self-imposed limitations from ourselves.

> **"... well, what's holding you back?"**

Conducting a personal SWOT analysis can be incredibly helpful. This structured method involves examining four key areas: strengths, weaknesses, opportunities, and threats. By identifying your strengths and weaknesses, you gain a clear understanding of what you excel at and where you need improvement. Looking at opportunities and threats helps you see external factors that could either aid or hinder your progress. This approach offers a more objective view of your limitations, especially in professional settings, by breaking down complex issues into manageable parts.

Complementing the SWOT analysis with mind mapping can provide an even clearer picture. Mind mapping is a visual tool where you draw a diagram with your main goal at the center, branching out into all the tasks, challenges, and sub-goals associated with it. This method helps you see how everything is connected and can highlight specific limitations, including those that are less obvious. By mapping out your goals and the obstacles in your way, you can more easily identify where you might need additional resources or support.

Reflecting on past experiences, especially those where we felt stuck or unsuccessful, can also be enlightening. Analyzing these situations with the benefit of hindsight can shed light on limitations that were not apparent at the time. Comparative analysis, where we measure our progress and approaches against those of individuals we admire in our field, can help identify what limitations we might have that they seem to overcome. This isn't about judging ourselves harshly but about pinpointing areas for growth.

By employing a combination of these techniques, we can develop a more comprehensive understanding of our limitations. This process calls for openness and a willingness to confront sometimes uncomfortable truths. Identifying our limitations is a critical step on the path to personal and professional development, and gaining this perspective from an external viewpoint can be a key to unlocking new avenues for growth and achievement.

Learn from Limits

Having explored how to identify your limitations, it's now crucial to shift our focus towards learning from them. This step is more than a means to overcoming obstacles; it is a vital process that fosters resilience and adaptability, key components of personal and professional growth.

Every limitation we encounter carries a lesson within it. For instance, a personal limitation I once faced was the fear of public speaking. In 2005 after graduating with an associate's degree in computer information systems I was asked to speak at graduation. At the time, the very idea of speaking in front of a large audience filled me with an overwhelming sense of fear. Public speaking was, for me, a challenging endeavor, one that stirred deep-seated anxieties and self-doubt. So, when the opportunity presented itself, my immediate reaction was to decline. The fear of potential embarrassment and the discomfort of standing before my peers and their families were barriers too great to overcome. At that moment, the decision to say no felt like a relief, a way to shield myself from my fears.

However, not long after making that decision, a sense of regret began to take root. The realization of what I had turned down — what I had let my fear steal from me — was a complete wake-up call. It wasn't just an opportunity to speak; it was an opportunity to overcome my fears, to grow, and to share a moment of triumph with those who had supported me throughout my academic journey. By the time I built up the courage to see if the offer still stood, it was too late. The opportunity had been given to someone else.

This experience, though initially filled with disappointment, became a pivotal moment in my life. It taught me a valuable lesson about the cost of letting fear dictate my actions. I promised myself that I would never again allow fear to stand in the way of an opportunity. This resolve has since guided my decisions, pushing me to embrace challenges and opportunities even when fear lurks in the background.

From this episode, I learned that fear, while a natural response, should not have the final say in our decisions. The growth that comes from stepping out of our comfort zone, from facing our fears head-on, is invaluable. This lesson, learned not through success but through a missed opportunity, has been instrumental in shaping my approach to life's challenges.

Reflecting on how past limitations have shaped your decisions and approaches is an insightful exercise. This isn't about lingering on past failures or challenges but rather understanding how your responses to these limitations have molded your character and skill set. It's in these moments of reflection that we often find the most profound insights into our personal growth journey.

The ability to adapt is crucial in our ever-evolving world, and learning from your limitations cultivates this adaptability. It prepares you to be flexible in your strategies, ensuring that you can navigate through various circumstances while staying focused on your goals. Adaptability is about adjusting based on past experiences and current realities, a skill sharpened through learning from every barrier you face.

A growth mindset plays a fundamental role in this learning process. Viewing limitations as opportunities for development and innovation, rather than permanent setbacks, encourages risk-taking, challenge-embracing, and viewing failure as a necessary step on the path to success. With a growth mindset, limitations become gateways to greater achievements.

Each limitation you overcome or learn from contributes significantly to your pool of experience and wisdom. This knowledge becomes a foundational layer for future projects and ventures. It helps you build more effective strategies, avoid repeating past mistakes, and approach new goals with an informed and confident mindset. In essence, learning from limitations prepares you for a cycle of continuous growth and success, turning every challenge into an opportunity for personal and professional development.

Embracing Unlimited Potential

The journey of understanding and overcoming our limitations leads to a powerful realization: the potential within us is unlimited. It's a call to action for you to see beyond the barriers, real or perceived, and to embrace the vast area of your capabilities.

The limitations you've encountered, no matter how overwhelming they may have seemed, are not the endpoints of your journey. Instead, see them as markers, directing you toward opportunities for growth, learning, and exploration. Every challenge you face and every obstacle you overcome adds to your resilience, broadens your perspective, and enhances your ability to tackle even greater challenges ahead.

As you move forward, let this realization empower you. When faced with a new limitation or an old fear, ask yourself: "Is this truly a barrier, or is it an opportunity for growth?" Use your newfound understanding and perspective to turn these challenges into opportunities that bring you closer to your goals.

> *"Is this truly a barrier, or is it an opportunity for growth?"*

Embrace each new experience, each new challenge, as a chance to expand your horizons and to test the waters of your potential. The journey of personal and professional growth is ongoing and constantly changing. There will always be new limitations to confront and new challenges to overcome. But with each step, you will discover more about yourself and what you can achieve. The path ahead is yours to shape, filled with unlimited possibilities and opportunities for growth and success.

Chapter 6:
The Resilient Path

Resilience is an essential quality, often misunderstood as merely enduring hardship. However, it's much more complex and powerful. It's the ability to withstand adversity, adapt to change, and emerge stronger from challenges. Resilience isn't about passively enduring; it's about actively growing through life's obstacles.

In facing life's challenges, whether personal or professional, resilience acts as a buffer against despair and defeat. It's the inner strength that enables us to navigate through tough times, learn from them, and bounce back with increased strength. This quality is crucial in all spheres of life, from overcoming personal tragedies to handling professional setbacks. It's about maintaining a positive attitude even when things don't go as planned and finding ways to turn setbacks into comebacks.

Resilience also plays a significant role in personal growth. Each challenge we face and overcome contributes to our resilience, making us better equipped to handle future difficulties. It helps us develop a deeper understanding of ourselves, our values, and our capabilities. In the professional realm, resilience is key to enduring the inevitable ups and downs of a career. It's about adapting to new situations, learning from failures, and continuously striving for improvement.

Furthermore, resilient individuals tend to be more optimistic, flexible, and proactive. They possess a unique ability to find solutions in the face of problems and are often seen as reliable and strong leaders. They inspire those around them through their perseverance and ability to turn challenges into opportunities for growth.

In essence, understanding and developing resilience is not just about surviving life's storms; it's about learning to thrive despite them. It's a dynamic process that involves self-awareness, self-care, and a positive mindset. Resilient individuals don't just recover from hardships; they use these experiences to grow stronger, wiser, and more empathetic.

The Roots of Resilience

Understanding where resilience comes from is essential to harnessing and nurturing it. Resilience is not a natural trait that only some people are born with; instead, it is a set of skills and habits that anyone can develop and strengthen over time. The roots of resilience are deeply embedded in a combination of personal experiences, mindset, and external influences.

One's life experiences play a crucial role in shaping resilience. It's often through facing and overcoming difficulties that individuals learn resilience. For example, overcoming a personal crisis, such as a health scare or a family issue, can build resilience. These experiences teach valuable lessons about coping and provide a sense of mastery over adversity. They also instill an understanding that challenges can be overcome, strengthening an individual's ability to face future hurdles.

The mindset with which one approaches life plays a key role in building resilience. Having a growth mindset means being willing to take on challenges, not giving up when faced with obstacles, understanding that effort is what leads to mastery, being open to learning from criticism, and finding inspiration in the success of others. This approach to life transforms obstacles into opportunities to learn and grow, fostering resilience.

External factors, such as the support system one has, also contribute significantly to resilience. Having a strong network of supportive family, friends, and colleagues can provide the encouragement and perspective needed to overcome challenges. These relationships can offer practical assistance, emotional support, and advice. Moreover, observing and learning from resilient role models can inspire and teach resilience strategies.

Resilience is also influenced by cultural, community, and societal factors. Different cultures have various ways of dealing with adversity; some may emphasize community support, while others might focus on individual grit. Growing up in a supportive community that encourages overcoming hardships can foster resilience from a young age.

Additionally, resilience is not constant; it can fluctuate over time and across different areas of life. Someone might display strong resilience in their professional life but find it challenging to do so in their personal life, or the other way around. This contrast underscores the importance of ongoing personal development and the need to strengthen resilience across all areas of life.

Resilience in Action

Resilience is best illustrated through action, particularly in how individuals respond to and overcome setbacks. One compelling chapter of resilience from my own journey through the business world unfolded after I took the leap of faith in launching my software company. What I hadn't anticipated was how a profound lack of business management knowledge would quickly surface as my most difficult challenge.

Compounded by marketing issues that led to a distressing decline in new clients, the survival of my hopeful venture hung in the balance. This unfortunate situation necessitated a temporary return to a previous employer, a humbling measure to ensure financial stability for my family while striving to keep my entrepreneurial dream afloat.

The very real possibility of business closure became increasingly likely, testing my determination to its limits. Yet, these trials proved to be invaluable learning opportunities. Confronting each issue, from refining marketing strategies to gaining essential business insight, not only prevented the downfall of my company but also significantly strengthened my resilience.

This ordeal, marked by its intense lessons on business management, client relations, and the critical nature of adaptability, transformed what were initially overwhelming challenges into vital growth opportunities. By facing and overcoming these adversities, I emerged with newfound insights and skills, laying a stronger foundation for my business and embarking on a path toward sustainable success.

Among many other tales of resilience, Diana Nyad's stands out prominently. At the age of 64, Nyad achieved an extraordinary feat that she had first attempted and failed at in her 20s. She became the first person to swim from Cuba to Florida without a shark cage, covering an incredible distance of over 100 miles in shark-infested waters, battling through severe jellyfish stings and extreme fatigue. This triumph came after four previous attempts, each hindered by various unbeatable obstacles. Despite the challenges, Nyad's relentless determination and her mantra, "Find a way," drove her to achieve her lifelong dream. Her story is a powerful reminder that age and past failures do not define our abilities, and that with steadfast commitment, even the toughest challenges can be conquered.

Steve Jobs' journey with Apple represents a profound narrative of resilience. After being forced out from the company he co-founded in 1985, Jobs didn't see it as defeat but as an opportunity for growth. He founded NeXT, a venture that, while initially struggling, laid the groundwork for future innovations. Apple's acquisition of NeXT marked Jobs' return, leading to a revival that brought about revolutionary products like the iPod and iPhone, transforming the tech industry and changing consumer habits globally. Jobs' ability to bounce back from setbacks, seeing each as an opportunity rather than a roadblock, marked a turning point that propelled Apple to remarkable success, showcasing the lasting power of resilience.

Jesus Christ's life demonstrates extraordinary resilience, marked by His steadfast commitment to His divine mission, despite knowing the immense trials and ultimate sacrifice that awaited Him. From facing skepticism and outright hostility from religious authorities to enduring the betrayal of a close disciple, Jesus navigated each hurdle with grace and steadfast purpose. His ministry, filled with teachings, miracles, and acts of compassion, never faltered in the face of adversity. Instead, He embraced each challenge, using it as an opportunity to demonstrate love, forgiveness, and the strength of faith. Jesus's journey to the cross, burdened with the weight of humanity's sins, showcased a profound resilience rooted in trust in His Father's will and a deep love for mankind. Even in His final moments, Jesus's focus remained on the redemption and salvation of others, embodying the ultimate example of enduring strength and selfless resilience. His resurrection stands as a triumphant climax to His earthly journey, symbolizing victory over suffering and death and offering hope and inspiration for countless generations to follow.

These stories show how setbacks, whether personal or professional, can spark growth and transformation. They illustrate that resilience is not about avoiding difficulties but about facing them head-on, learning, and emerging stronger. They serve as powerful reminders that resilience is an active, dynamic process – one that involves facing challenges, adapting, and continually moving forward.

Building Resilience

Developing resilience is like building muscle; it requires consistent practice, persistence, and the right approach. This part of the journey focuses on practical strategies and tools to help build and reinforce resilience, including mindset adjustments, coping techniques, and strengthening your determination.

A fundamental aspect of building resilience is a shift in mindset. This shift involves embracing a growth mindset, seeing challenges not as overwhelming obstacles but as opportunities for development. It entails reframing setbacks as learning experiences rather than failures. This change in perspective alters how we react to challenges, helping us uncover valuable lessons in difficult situations. Understanding that setbacks are a natural part of life and career paths, and accepting this reality, allows us to face challenges more calmly and balanced.

Effective coping mechanisms are crucial in building resilience. Stress management techniques such as mindfulness, meditation, and deep breathing exercises can help manage stress and anxiety, often side effects of setbacks. Journaling about experiences, especially challenging ones, provides emotional release and perspective. Building a supportive network, be it friends, family, mentors, or professional counselors, can provide a pillar of strength, encouragement, and guidance.

Strengthening your perseverance requires consistent effort and a willingness to face and overcome smaller challenges along the way. Each time you confront a difficulty and push through, you build resilience. Observing how others have managed tough situations can provide valuable insights and practical strategies. Engaging in continuous learning, whether through formal education, workshops, or self-study, sharpens your mind and enhances your ability to adapt to change.

Emotional resilience is as crucial as mental toughness. This involves developing self-compassion and being kind to oneself in moments of failure or difficulty. Self-compassion fosters emotional resilience, enabling quicker recovery from setbacks. Practicing gratitude, as well as regularly acknowledging and appreciating what's going well, shifts focus from what's going wrong, building a buffer against despair and hopelessness. Improving emotional intelligence, which involves recognizing, understanding, and managing emotions, enhances our capacity to navigate life's highs and lows with grace.

Physical resilience also plays a vital role. Regular exercise is not only beneficial for health but also mental well-being. Exercise releases endorphins, which have mood-boosting properties. Proper rest and nutrition are foundational for mental and physical resilience. They maintain energy levels and cognitive function.

Integrating these tools and strategies into daily life can gradually build and strengthen resilience. It's a journey of small steps, where each challenge faced and overcome contributes to a more resilient mindset and approach to life. Just like muscles grow stronger with consistent training, so does our ability to bounce back from setbacks and face future challenges with confidence and determination.

The Power of a Resilient Mindset

Embarking on the path to developing a resilient mindset involves reshaping our approach to life's obstacles and setbacks. This mindset isn't just about enduring difficulties; it's about transforming the way we perceive and engage with challenges. A resilient mindset embodies a problem-solving attitude, one that finds lessons and opportunities in every setback.

The power of a resilient mindset lies in its proactive nature. Instead of being reactive to challenges, individuals with a resilient mindset anticipate potential hurdles and approach them with strategies and adaptability. This forward-thinking approach allows for better preparation and a more composed response when difficulties arise. It's about expecting the unexpected and having a plan, or at least a mindset, ready to tackle it.

A key characteristic of a resilient mindset is its focus on learning. Every setback is seen as a learning opportunity, a chance to gather insights that can inform future decisions and actions. This learning-focused approach shifts the narrative from "I failed" to "I learned." It turns experiences, even the painful ones, into valuable lessons. For instance, a failed business venture becomes a masterclass in what to do differently next time, rather than a defining moment of defeat.

Moreover, a resilient mindset is characterized by flexibility and adaptability. It recognizes a fixed mindset can be a barrier to overcoming challenges. Those who build resilience are open to changing their approach, adapting their methods, and even shifting their goals as circumstances evolve. They understand that sometimes the path to success is not linear and requires pivoting or taking detours.

Another significant aspect of a resilient mindset is persistence. This doesn't mean relentlessly pushing without regard to reality but rather a steadfast commitment to one's goals, even in the face of setbacks. It's about not giving up at the first sign of difficulty but instead, finding ways to persevere. This persistence is coupled with a realistic optimism – a belief that things can improve and that efforts will eventually yield results, even if the path is challenging.

In essence, a resilient mindset equips individuals with a toolkit to face life's challenges head-on. It's a mindset that embraces problems as opportunities for growth, that learns from every experience, and that adapts and persists despite difficulties. By adopting this mindset, obstacles become less intimidating, and the journey, with all its ups and downs, becomes a more enriching experience.

Embracing Change

In the realm of personal and professional development, resilience and adaptability emerge as crucial for navigating life's ever-changing challenges. Resilience isn't merely about recovering from setbacks; it's using these challenges as springboards for growth. Adaptability, on the other hand, is the ability to adjust one's approach in response to new situations, a skill equally as vital as resilience. Together, they create a formidable pair for embracing change.

Resilience provides the strength to endure adversities, while adaptability ensures the agility to evolve with changing circumstances. In today's rapidly evolving world, where change is constant and inevitable, embracing this reality is critical. Individuals who see change as an opportunity rather than a threat often emerge more robust and skilled. It's about transforming the overwhelming into intriguing puzzles to solve and perceiving every new situation as a chance to learn. This approach not only makes adaptability less intimidating but also enriches the journey.

Consider, for instance, the numerous businesses that faced extraordinary challenges during the COVID-19 pandemic, which threatened their very foundations. Restaurants, retail stores, and service providers found themselves dealing with a reality where traditional models were no longer viable. For many, the necessary detour came in the form of pivoting their business models to adapt to the rapidly changing market landscape—a move that was not part of the original plan.

Restaurants, for example, shifted to takeout and delivery services, often partnering with food delivery apps and rethinking their menus to accommodate off-premises dining. Retail stores moved online, accelerating their digital transformation to offer e-commerce solutions, virtual shopping experiences, and curbside pickups. Service providers turned to virtual platforms, conducting consultations, classes, and events through video conferencing tools.

These pivots not only saved many businesses from closure but also pushed them to new heights, uncovering previously unimagined potential. Some restaurants discovered a broader customer base through delivery services, leading to higher sales volumes than before. Retailers who had been hesitant to embrace e-commerce found themselves thriving in the digital marketplace, reaching customers far beyond their local areas. Service providers expanded their client base globally, as virtual services eliminated geographical limitations.

It was the flexibility and willingness to adapt that turned what seemed like dire situations into opportunities for greater success. Businesses that embraced change and innovation were able to navigate the challenges, reinvent their operations, and find new avenues for growth. This period of rapid adaptation highlighted the importance of resilience and creativity in overcoming obstacles and thriving in the face of adversity.

Being flexible means letting go of rigid expectations and understanding that success is not always a linear process. It involves being open to reassessing our goals, methods, and even our definitions of success as we encounter new information and experiences. This flexibility doesn't mean losing sight of our dreams but rather being willing to find alternative routes to reach them.

Adaptability also requires a certain level of resilience and optimism. It's about facing the unknown with a belief in our ability to navigate through it and come out stronger on the other side. It's about seeing change not as a threat but as an integral part of life's adventure—a series of chapters that contribute to our story in ways we might never have imagined.

Let us embrace the concept of adaptability as a core component of our growth. Let's approach life's detours with curiosity and openness, understanding that while they may take us on paths we didn't plan, they also offer us the chance to see the world, and ourselves, from perspectives we might have otherwise missed. In doing so, we cultivate a life rich with experiences, learning, and the joy of discovery, fully embracing the infinite possibilities that come with the willingness to adapt.

The Future Path

Building resilience is not a destination to be reached, but a pathway to be navigated, continually shaped by our experiences, learning, and growth. As we look to the future, understanding that resilience is a lifelong journey is vital in preparing us to face the multitude of challenges that life inevitably presents.

Each stage of life brings its unique trials and triumphs, and with them, the opportunity to reinforce our resilience. Just as a river carves its path through the landscape over time, so too does our resilience deepen and expand with each experience. The future, with all its uncertainties and potential, is a landscape where our resilience shapes a story of strength, adaptability, and growth.

In the coming years, our resilience may be tested in ways we can't currently imagine. Technological advancements, social and economic shifts, personal transitions, and unforeseen global events all have the potential to challenge us in profound ways. These challenges, however, are not merely obstacles; they are opportunities to apply our resilience, to learn from new situations, and to adapt our strategies and perspectives.

Imagine the future as a series of gates, each leading to new experiences and opportunities. As we pass through them, we carry with us the lessons and strengths gained from previous challenges. Our resilience, honed through past experiences, prepares us to face these new scenarios with a sense of confidence and capability. With each challenge we overcome, our resilience becomes more ingrained, more a part of who we are and how we approach the world.

Moreover, the future of resilience is not just about individual strength. It's about how our personal resilience contributes to the resilience of our communities, workplaces, and societies. The challenges of the future will require collective resilience – the ability to work together, to support each other, and to bounce back from collective setbacks stronger than before.

As we embrace this lifelong journey of resilience, we should be mindful of its evolving nature. The resilience we build today may look different from the resilience we'll need ten or twenty years from now. This evolution is a natural and necessary part of growth. It requires an openness to continual learning, a willingness to adapt, and a recognition that the journey of resilience is as dynamic as life itself.

In essence, the future path of resilience is about embracing the unknown with the knowledge that we have built a foundation strong enough to support us. It's about looking forward to the possibilities that lie ahead, knowing that with each challenge comes the opportunity to strengthen and redefine our resilience. As we navigate this path, we can take comfort in knowing that our resilience is a companion that grows and adapts with us, a steadfast ally in the journey of life.

Chapter 7: Embracing the Journey

In our journey toward achieving our goals and aspirations, it's crucial to recognize the true beauty and value of the process itself. Often, we become so fixated on the destination – the final achievement or the peak of our efforts – that we overlook the richness and fulfillment found in the journey. It's in the journey where we find growth, learning, and the joy of discovery, which are just as important as the end goal.

Take, for instance, the analogy of climbing a mountain. The true essence of this endeavor isn't merely in reaching the peak; it's in the climb. With each step upwards, climbers are met with challenges that test their resolve and strength, yet they are also rewarded with breathtaking views and unique experiences that the summit alone cannot offer. The peak, though a significant achievement, is but a passing moment, whereas the climb is an enduring journey of self-discovery and perseverance.

Similarly, consider the dedication and resilience involved in learning to play a musical instrument. The true achievement isn't just in performing a flawless piece but in the countless hours spent practicing scales, mastering techniques, and working through challenging passages. Each note played and each skill acquired reflects the musician's perseverance and commitment. The journey is filled with moments of frustration and breakthrough, discipline, and discovery. The fulfillment comes not just from the final performance, but from the entire process of growth and learning that leads to it.

Another beautiful example can be seen in gardening. The joy derived from this activity goes beyond the blooming flowers or the harvested produce. It lies in daily nurturing – the watering, pruning, and caring for the plants. Gardeners find pleasure in the act of tending to their garden, observing the subtle changes and growth each day brings. This daily commitment to nurturing life offers a unique sense of satisfaction that goes beyond the final outcome.

Through these examples, we see that embracing the journey is about finding value and joy in every part of the process. It's about learning to love the path with all its ups and downs, triumphs and challenges, as much as we cherish the destination. Adopting this mindset transforms our approach to our goals and dreams. It turns every phase of our journey into an opportunity for joy, fulfillment, and meaningful experiences. When we learn to embrace the journey, we open ourselves to a fuller, more enriching path toward our aspirations, where every step holds its own unique beauty and significance.

Lessons Along the Path

Life's journey is filled with moments that, at first glance, may seem ordinary or insignificant, but they carry within them the seeds of growth and transformation. These moments, whether they bring joy or challenge, are the true markers of our personal development.

Some of the most valuable lessons are those we learn in unexpected ways. For example, you may find that what seemed like a small decision at the time had far-reaching consequences, teaching you about the power of choice and the importance of being intentional in your actions. Perhaps you've experienced the frustration of repeated efforts that didn't generate immediate results, only to later realize that persistence was quietly building your resilience and strength.

There are also the lessons learned from others—those who have walked similar paths and shared their wisdom with us. We learn the importance of mentorship and community, understanding that we don't have to navigate our journey alone. Observing the successes and setbacks of others can offer us a map for our own path, helping us avoid pitfalls and recognize opportunities that might otherwise go unnoticed.

Likewise, there are the lessons that come from moments of stillness and reflection. In a world that often prioritizes speed and efficiency, it's easy to overlook the value of slowing down and taking stock of where we are. These quiet moments allow us to process our experiences, gain clarity, and reconnect with our purpose. It's in these pauses that we often find the answers we've been searching for.

As you reflect on your own journey, consider the lessons you've gathered along the way. Each step, whether it led to success or a learning experience, has contributed to your growth. Embrace these lessons with gratitude, knowing that they have shaped you into the person you are today and will continue to guide you toward who you are becoming.

Remember, the path you are on is unique to you, and every lesson learned is a step forward. As you continue to move through life, let these insights serve as your compass, helping you navigate the road ahead with confidence, wisdom, and an open heart.

The Power of Persistence

Persistence is an essential quality that fills our journey with the strength and resilience necessary to navigate life's challenges. It's the firm dedication to our path, the driving force that pushes us forward through uncertainty, doubt, and the inevitable setbacks that accompany any meaningful endeavor. In the realm of personal and professional growth, persistence is not just a strategy; it's a fundamental aspect of character that defines our ability to achieve our goals and actualize our dreams.

The essence of persistence lies in its simplicity and its complexity. It's the simple act of continuing despite difficulty or delay in achieving success. Yet, within this simple action lies a complex combination of motivation, belief, and courage. Persistence asks us to hold fast to our vision, to believe in our ability to overcome obstacles, and to have the courage to face failure without being defined by it.

Persistence is born from a deep place within us—a place of passion, purpose, and a strong belief in our path. It's fueled by a core understanding that the journey towards any worthwhile goal is filled with challenges, and it's these very challenges that make the journey worthwhile. This understanding allows us to approach obstacles with a problem-solving attitude, finding lessons in every setback and opportunities in every failure.

Developing tenacity, a close ally to persistence, involves recognizing that every step taken, no matter how small, is a step toward our goals. It's understanding that the path to success is not a straight line, but a winding road filled with peaks and valleys. The key is to keep moving, to find value in every experience, and to use our setbacks as fuel for our journey forward.

The power of a resilient mindset becomes evident in our approach to challenges. With persistence, obstacles become opportunities to learn and grow. Setbacks become moments of reflection and recalibration. Each failure brings us closer to success, not by diminishing the value of our efforts, but by enriching our journey with invaluable lessons and experiences.

In essence, persistence is a testament to our belief in ourselves and our dreams. It reflects our commitment to our path and willingness to invest in our own growth. As we continue our journey, let us embrace persistence not just as a means to an end, but as a defining element of our path—a force that empowers us to approach every challenge with confidence, to learn from every setback, and to move forward with unshakable determination toward our ultimate destination.

Redefining Success

As we journey through life, the concept of success often shapes our direction and decisions. However, just as the journey itself evolves, so should our understanding of what success truly means. We must recognize that success isn't a fixed point or a one-size-fits-all achievement—it's a deeply personal, evolving concept that should align with our values and experiences along the way.

Success is often framed by external standards—societal expectations, cultural norms, or the accomplishments of others. These influences can lead us to pursue goals that may not genuinely resonate with our own aspirations. But when we chase a version of success that's defined by others, we risk losing sight of what really matters to us. This can lead to an empty feeling, even when we accomplish what we set out to do.

A key to achieving success is taking the time to define success on your own terms. It's not just about reaching a destination or hitting a milestone. It's about finding meaning and satisfaction in the process—in the steps you take, the challenges you overcome, and the growth you experience along the way. Success could be about pursuing a passion, nurturing relationships, making a positive impact, or simply maintaining a healthy balance in your life.

As you continue your journey, it's important to allow your definition of success to evolve. What you value today might change tomorrow, and that's okay. By staying flexible and true to yourself, you ensure that your goals remain aligned with your current values and priorities, making the journey itself more fulfilling.

Redefining success also means letting go of the fear of judgment from others. The journey is yours to walk, and only you can determine what success looks like for you. By focusing on your own path and celebrating each step forward, you create a sense of accomplishment that's rooted in personal growth, rather than external validation.

Ultimately, redefining success as part of your journey allows you to live a life that's true to who you are. It's a reminder that success isn't a static goal, but a dynamic, ongoing process that's intertwined with your personal growth and self-discovery. By embracing this perspective, you not only enrich your journey but also create a lasting sense of fulfillment and purpose.

The Destination as a Moving Target

Our goals and aspirations are like moving targets, continuously evolving with our growth, learning, and the paths we navigate. This dynamic process of change is not merely incidental; it's a crucial aspect of our journey, mirroring our deepening self-awareness and expanding worldview. Recognizing that our end goals are subject to change underscores our natural ability to grow and adapt, highlighting the transformative power of the journey itself.

The essence of our journey isn't captured solely in reaching specific destinations but is woven into the diverse experiences, lessons, and personal transformations we encounter along the way. Each step on this path offers profound learning opportunities, testing and refining our character in invaluable ways. This understanding releases us from rigidly clinging to initial plans, which may no longer resonate with who we have become. It allows our goals to mature and shift, keeping them in harmony with our evolving values and true selves.

Moreover, this perspective alleviates the sting of frustration or feelings of failure when life inevitably steers us in unexpected directions. Rather than viewing these moments as detours from success, they're embraced as fundamental milestones in a broader narrative of self-discovery and achievement. Success, therefore, is not perceived as a singular, unchanging destination but as a series of significant achievements that together sculpt the contours of our journey.

This fluid approach to our aspirations invites us to welcome new possibilities and adapt our goals with the insights and experiences life gives us. It's an affirmation that our aspirations, like us, are meant to grow, suggesting that flexibility in our goals is a hallmark of our commitment to continual self-improvement and satisfaction.

Let this perspective guide us as we navigate the ever-shifting landscape of life: "The start and the finish are important in determining success, but it's the in-between where the true essence of our journey unfolds." It serves as a powerful reminder that each step, filled with its own set of challenges and victories, contributes to our overarching narrative of growth. In pursuing these evolving ambitions, we encounter our most valuable lessons and achieve our deepest fulfillment.

> *"The start and the finish are important in determining success, but it's the in-between where the true essence of our journey unfolds."*

Let us embrace the notion that our objectives will transform alongside us. By doing so, we celebrate not just the goals themselves but the journey towards them, honoring the ever-changing nature of our dreams and the boundless opportunities for discovery that lie ahead.

The Unending Road of Self-Discovery

In this life journey, growth is an unending process, a continuous path of self-discovery that we tread upon daily. It is a voyage that doesn't have a final destination, for with every step forward, we uncover new layers about ourselves, our desires, our fears, and our untapped potential. This realization—that growth is unending—is vital to not just embracing every aspect of our journey but also to appreciating the beauty and lessons it offers along the way.

Understanding that ongoing growth encourages us to remain curious, open, and adaptable. It teaches us that who we were yesterday doesn't have to define who we will be tomorrow, and that our past experiences are not constraints but opportunities for learning. It's in this ever-evolving narrative of our lives that we find the freedom to explore, make mistakes, learn, and redefine our paths as many times as necessary.

Embracing every aspect of this journey means acknowledging that there will be highs and lows, successes and setbacks, and that each of these experiences contributes to our growth. It's about learning to value the process as much as, if not more than, the outcomes. By doing so, we allow ourselves to live fully in each moment, extracting wisdom and strength from our challenges and using them to propel us forward.

This ongoing process of self-discovery asks us to be patient and kind to ourselves. It requires us to celebrate our victories, no matter how small, and to extend compassion to ourselves in our moments of struggle. It reminds us that growth is not linear, nor is it always comfortable, but it is always, without fail, moving us closer to our authentic selves.

As we reflect on the journey thus far, let us hold onto the understanding that the road of self-discovery is unending. Let's approach each new day with a sense of wonder and readiness to learn, grow, and evolve. Let us embrace the entirety of our journey with gratitude, knowing that each step, each experience, and each moment of reflection adds to the richness of our lives.

In recognizing that growth is an ongoing process, we free ourselves from the pressure of reaching a final form or destination. Instead, we open ourselves up to a lifetime of learning, evolving, and becoming. This is the essence of the unending road of self-discovery—a path that invites us to explore endlessly, to embrace change, and to continually find new ways to flourish and shine.

As we move forward, let this understanding guide our steps, encouraging us to embrace every aspect of our growth with open arms and an eager heart. It is in this journey of constant becoming that we find our truest selves and our deepest sense of fulfillment.

Chapter 8:
The "Yet Mindset"

At the heart of every challenge, setback, or perceived failure lies a powerful three-letter word that holds the key to unlocking our true potential: "yet." This simple conjunction, often overlooked in our daily vocabulary, serves as a bridge between the present and the future, between our current state and our limitless possibilities. The "yet mindset" is not just an optimistic way to view the world; it's a fundamental shift in how we approach our goals, challenges, and the process of learning itself. It transforms the fixed barriers of our capabilities into milestones of our growth journey, emphasizing that while we may not have achieved something now, the potential for success lies just on the horizon.

Understanding the "yet mindset" begins with recognizing that our journey toward personal and professional development is ongoing. It reminds us that our current limitations are not permanent but rather temporary states awaiting transformation through effort, perseverance, and the passage of time. This mindset encourages us to view every "not yet" as an opportunity for growth, a challenge to embrace, and a future success story in the making. It teaches us that every "can't" is merely a "can" that hasn't happened yet, shifting our focus from what we lack to what we are striving to achieve.

Embracing the "yet mindset" is about understanding that the path to mastery is paved with trials, errors, and lessons learned. It's about seeing the beauty in the process of becoming, acknowledging that every skill we wish to acquire and every goal we aim to reach is within our grasp, given time and persistence. This mindset encourages the idea that our abilities are not fixed traits but evolving qualities that can be nurtured and developed through dedication and hard work.

In diving into the understanding of the "yet mindset," we embark on a journey that redefines our relationship with failure, success, and the pursuit of our ambitions. It invites us to adopt a perspective that sees beyond the immediate hurdles, focusing instead on the endless possibilities that await us. The "yet mindset" is a powerful testament to the human spirit's resilience, reminding us that with each "not yet" we encounter, we are one step closer to realizing our full potential.

The Power of "Yet"

Incorporating the word "yet" into our vocabulary does more than just add a temporal dimension to our statements—it fundamentally alters the way we think and approach challenges. This seemingly simple linguistic tweak has the power to shift our mindset from one that is fixed and static to one that is growth-oriented and dynamic. The essence of this shift lies in how we perceive our abilities and challenges, transforming our approach to learning, problem-solving, and personal development.

The concept of "yet" is deeply rooted in the principles of a growth mindset, which suggests our abilities and intelligence can be developed with time, effort, and perseverance. This mindset contrasts with a fixed mindset, where abilities are seen as natural and unchangeable. When faced with challenges or learning new skills, those with a fixed mindset might declare, "I can't do this," viewing their limitations as permanent. However, by adding "yet" to this statement, "I can't do this...yet," we open ourselves up to the possibility of growth and improvement. This small linguistic shift signifies a profound change in how we view our potential: no longer static, but constantly evolving.

The power of "yet" extends beyond mere positive thinking; it taps into the foundational principles of neuroplasticity, which is the brain's capacity to form new neural connections throughout life. This understanding that our brain and abilities are not fixed, but flexible and responsive to our actions, reinforces the mindset that with effort and persistence, improvement and mastery are within reach. "Yet" becomes a bridge between our current state and our potential, emphasizing that the journey to acquiring new skills or overcoming obstacles is part of an ongoing process of learning and growth.

Additionally, adopting a "yet mindset" impacts not just our self-perception but also how we interact with the world around us. It builds resilience in the face of setbacks, promoting a persistence rooted in the understanding that failure is not a permanent state but a temporary hurdle on the path to mastery. This shift in perspective nurtures a love for learning, as challenges are no longer seen as threats to our self-esteem but as opportunities to expand our knowledge and abilities.

Adopting the "yet mindset" also reshapes our internal dialogue, turning self-limiting beliefs into affirmations of potential. It teaches us to counteract thoughts of doubt and limitation with the promise of progress and development. This change in our internal narrative is crucial, as it directly impacts our motivation, engagement, and resilience. By framing our goals and challenges with "yet," we maintain a forward-looking perspective, one that is oriented towards solutions and growth rather than obstacles and inaction.

In essence, the power of "yet" is a testament to the transformative influence of language and mindset on our perception of self and our interaction with the world. It underscores the importance of embracing a growth mindset, where the focus shifts from proving our intelligence or talent to developing them. "Yet" is a constant reminder that our current limitations are merely starting points for our journey toward growth and achievement. This mindset not only changes how we approach learning and development but also profoundly influences our overall sense of possibility and potential in life.

Stepping Out of Your Comfort Zone

Stepping out of your comfort zone is a transformative moment that marks the beginning of growth and self-improvement. It challenges the boundaries of what you believe is possible, urging you to embrace new opportunities and experiences with optimism and courage. While the comfort zone may feel like a safe harbor, it often serves as a subtle cage that restricts potential and hinders growth. This space, filled with routine and the familiar, creates a false sense of security, quietly sidelining dreams and aspirations in favor of the fear of the unknown.

The journey to stepping out of your comfort zone begins with embracing uncertainty, and acknowledging that the unknown, while intimidating, is also filled with potential. This shift in perspective turns fear into excitement, converting each new challenge into a chance for personal development. It's about recognizing beauty in the process of becoming more than you were yesterday and understanding that real learning and discovery lie just beyond the confines of comfort.

Building confidence is a crucial step in venturing beyond known boundaries. It starts with celebrating small wins and setting achievable goals that pave the way for greater self-assurance. Each victory, no matter its size, is a testament to your capabilities, slowly constructing a foundation of confidence that supports taking bolder steps. Incorporating the mindset of "yet" into this process is transformative; it serves as a powerful reminder that current limitations are not permanent but merely temporary challenges to future successes.

Actively seeking out new experiences is vital for pushing the limits of your comfort zone. Whether it's acquiring a new skill, exploring an unfamiliar place, or simply changing up your daily routine, each new endeavor is an opportunity to expand your horizons. It's these moments of stepping into the unknown, armed with the belief in your ability to overcome and adapt, that true growth occurs. Embracing the mindset of "yet" initiates a continuous cycle of trying, learning, and eventually mastering new challenges, proving to yourself that the only real limits are those you place on yourself.

Transforming Failure with Yet

Transforming one's perception of failure is essential in the journey toward personal and professional growth. Failure, often feared and avoided, is not the opposite of success but rather an integral part of the process leading to it. Adopting the "yet mindset" plays a crucial role in redefining failure, shifting it from an endpoint to a milestone on the path to achievement. This point of view promotes the notion that failure is not a permanent condition, but rather a momentary hindrance that indicates you have not achieved success—yet.

By embracing this mindset, every experience of failure becomes a lesson in disguise, an opportunity to reassess, learn, and improve. It's in these moments of reflection that the most valuable insights are gained, insights that refine strategies, strengthen resolve, and enhance understanding. Seeing failure through the lens of "yet" transforms it from a deterrent into a motivator, a signal that you're pushing boundaries and venturing into realms where success is not yet guaranteed but is certainly attainable with persistence and resilience.

Encouraging continuous forward movement, the "yet mindset" instills a sense of hope and possibility. It's a powerful reminder that the journey to success is a series of attempts, each one bringing you closer to your goals. This approach encourages a resilient mindset, one that sees setbacks not as reasons to quit but as motivation to push forward, innovate, and keep trying with the lessons learned from past experiences.

Additionally, this mindset nurtures an environment where the fear of failure fades, giving way to a bold drive to explore, experiment, and broaden one's capabilities. It's about understanding that every step forward, even those that appear to be setbacks, contributes to progress when seen through the lens of "yet." It reinforces the idea that success is not reserved for a select few but is attainable by anyone who is willing to persevere, learn from their mistakes, and keep striving with a steady belief in their eventual success.

In essence, transforming failure with "yet" is about shifting the narrative from one of limitations to one of limitless potential. It's a powerful affirmation that while you may not have succeeded in this moment, the journey is far from over. With each attempt, you're not only getting closer to your goals but also becoming a more resilient, knowledgeable, and capable individual. The "yet mindset" thus becomes not just a strategy for overcoming failure but a philosophy for life, infusing every challenge with the promise of eventual triumph.

Creating a "Yet Mindset" Culture

Creating a "Yet Mindset" Culture transcends personal development, morphing into a powerful tool for communal growth and support. When individuals embrace the transformative potential of "yet," they not only unlock their own capabilities but also spark change within their wider circles. By integrating the "yet mindset" into daily interactions with families, coworkers, and communities, a culture of resilience, innovation, and encouragement begins to flourish.

This cultural shift towards a "yet mindset" encourages environments where growth is not just encouraged but expected. In families, for instance, adopting this mindset can help children and adults alike view challenges as opportunities rather than obstacles. For example, in my own family, we have embraced the "yet mindset," and I've seen its transformative impact on my youngest daughter. She used to say, "I can't do this" or "I don't know how to do that," but now she confidently adds "yet" to her statements. Hearing her say, "I can't do this… yet" and "I don't know how to do that… yet," fills me with joy. This change has shifted her thinking from self-doubt to a new, empowered way of approaching challenges. Parents and guardians leading by example can instill a lifelong habit of resilience in young minds, teaching them that setbacks are merely temporary and that their potential is boundless.

In the workplace, a "yet mindset" culture transforms the approach to tasks, projects, and innovation. It encourages teams to push beyond their perceived limits, adopting a space where ideas are freely shared, and failures are seen as steps towards success. Managers and leaders who promote this mindset can drive their teams to greater achievements, creating an atmosphere where employees feel valued and inspired to explore their full potential.

Creating such a culture also means redefining how success and failure are perceived collectively. It involves celebrating attempts and efforts, not just outcomes, thereby removing the stigma associated with not reaching a goal on the first try. This shift can significantly impact how individuals approach their tasks and interact with each other, promoting a more collaborative and supportive environment.

Also, spreading the "yet mindset" within communities can ignite a collective spirit of endurance and ambition. Community projects, educational initiatives, and local businesses can all benefit from this shift in perspective. When communities begin to see their challenges through the lens of "yet," they open the door to a wealth of potential for collective action, innovation, and progress.

In essence, creating a "yet mindset" culture is about seeding a belief in endless possibilities, a conviction that no goal is too distant, and no dream is unattainable. It's about building networks of support that uplift every member and encourage taking risks, knowing that the path to success is paved with lessons learned from every setback. By embodying and spreading this mindset, individuals can inspire those around them to embrace their own journeys of growth and discovery, encouraging environments where everyone thrives together.

Chapter 9: Start the Finish

As we prepare to conclude this transformative journey, it's essential to look back at the terrain we've traversed, the challenges overcome, and the insights gained. Each chapter acted as a milestone, not just directing us toward our destination but also enriching us with invaluable lessons and empowering us to tackle the final leap: starting the finish.

The Starting Line

Our journey started right on the edge of action, where the anticipation of the path ahead was filled with possibilities. We embraced the spark that ignites the journey, understanding that every significant venture begins with the courage to take the first step.

The 80/20 Challenge

Exploring the Pareto Principle, we examined how most of our outcomes stem from a minimal portion of our efforts, and it's the challenging final stretch that truly defines our journey. This realization set the stage for the challenges and triumphs that awaited.

Ideas Without Action

We ventured into the realm of unactualized potential, confronting the silent graveyard of dreams never pursued. This chapter underscored the importance of action, breathing life into dormant dreams to transform them into tangible realities.

Silencing the Fear Within

Fear, in its many forms, was acknowledged as a significant challenge. We learned to recognize and disarm the fears of failure, success, judgment, and the unknown, reclaiming our power to move forward without restraint.

The Landscape of Limitations

Our exploration brought us face-to-face with the invisible barriers of self-imposed and external limitations. Recognizing these constraints revealed the path to overcoming them, unlocking our untapped potential.

The Resilient Path

Resilience emerged as our guiding light through adversity. This chapter celebrated resilience not as a natural trait but as a skill developed through facing setbacks, teaching us that true strength lies in our capacity to endure and evolve.

Embracing the Journey

We reflected on the essence of our voyage, recognizing that the true value lies not merely in reaching our goals but in cherishing the experiences and growth reached along the way.

The "Yet Mindset"

The transformative power of "yet" was uncovered, showing how this simple linguistic shift can reframe our outlook, encouraging a growth mindset that drives us toward endless possibilities.

As we stand on the brink of concluding this chapter of our lives, these insights signal us to forge ahead with a renewed spirit. The journey thus far has not just been about reaching a destination but about the transformation we've gone through, equipped with the knowledge that our endeavors, dreams, and aspirations are never truly finished; they merely evolve.

The Road to Completion

As we journey together through the winding paths of self-discovery, growth, and resilience, we arrive at a critical crossroads: the opportunity to revisit the endeavors we left unfinished, the dreams we shelved, and the projects we labeled as failures. This moment, right here, is your invitation to look back—not with regret, but with a renewed perspective and the powerful toolkit of insights and strategies you've collected along the way.

In every chapter of this book, from "The Starting Line" to "The Yet Mindset," we've explored the essence of pushing beyond our perceived limits, transforming our fears into opportunities, and embracing every setback as a lesson in disguise. Now, it's time to apply these lessons to the ventures you once paused, the goals you thought were out of reach, and the ideas that never made it past the drawing board.

Every moment presents a new opportunity to begin again, this time with more wisdom, more resilience, and a deeper understanding of your capabilities. Your unfinished symphony awaits its finale, and you hold the conductor's baton.

Think back to those past projects and dreams. What was it that made you halt? Was it fear of failure, a lack of resources, or perhaps a missing piece of knowledge or skill? Whatever the reason, view it through the lens of everything you've learned:

- **Resilience** is your newfound strength, teaching you that setbacks are merely pauses, not the end.
- **Adaptability** has shown you the power of pivoting, of finding new paths to the same destination.
- The **"Yet Mindset"** instills the belief that just because you haven't achieved it yet doesn't mean you won't.

This journey you're on is about rediscovering those closed doors and recognizing that now, equipped with a key forged from resilience, insight, and unwavering determination, you're ready to unlock them. Keep in mind that "every closed door contains an opportunity on the other side. You must decide if you want to open it."

> *"Every closed door contains an opportunity on the other side. You must decide if you want to open it."*

The Action Plan

At this stage of our journey together, having navigated through the landscapes of resilience, embracing the power of "yet," and rediscovering the dreams left on the wayside, we arrive at a crucial milestone: The Action Plan. This isn't merely a set of steps or tasks; it's your blueprint to turning the page from contemplation to action, from paused dreams to dynamic pursuits of completion.

The essence of this plan lies in its simplicity and clarity. It begins with revisiting those dreams and projects you've shelved. Select a goal that resonates deeply with your current aspirations and reflects the growth you've experienced through this journey. This selection process is not just about picking a task; it's about aligning with your most authentic self and the visions you hold for your future.

Once chosen, the next step is setting clear, achievable goals. These aren't just endpoints but milestones that mark your progress. Define what completion looks like for this project. Is it launching a business, finishing a manuscript, or perhaps mastering a skill? Whatever it is, visualize that moment of achievement clearly in your mind.

Breaking down tasks is your strategy to make this vision tangible. Every journey is comprised of steps, and every complex project can be divided into manageable tasks. List these tasks, understanding that each one is a step closer to your goal. This breakdown simplifies what may seem like an overwhelming endeavor and provides a clear path forward.

Scheduling actions is where your plan gains momentum. Assign realistic deadlines to each task, considering your current commitments and lifestyle. This schedule is your commitment to yourself, a reflection of the resilience and determination you've developed. It transforms your goal from a distant dream into a series of actionable steps.

Now, the challenge lies in taking that first step. Upon finishing this book, don't let the inspiration diminish or the motivation fade. Schedule your first action. Whether conducting research, writing a plan, or simply sketching ideas, make it a tangible task that marks the beginning of your journey to completion. Let this action be a declaration, a statement that you're not just planning but doing.

This Action Plan is more than a method; it's a commitment to yourself, a testament to your growth and the lessons learned throughout this book. It's a reminder that the path to achieving your dreams is paved with intentional actions, resilience in the face of setbacks, and the relentless pursuit of completion.

Let this plan be the spark that drives you from contemplation to action, turning your dreams into reality. Remember, no matter the distance, the journey must begin with a single step. Make that step count. Schedule it, commit to it, and let it be the first of many that will lead you to realize your dreams. You've explored the depths of what holds you back and discovered the heights of what you can achieve. Now, it's time to put that knowledge into action. The time is now; your next step awaits.

Start the Finish

As we reach the final pages of this journey, I want to leave you with a message of hope, resilience, and unyielding determination. Remember, your past does not define your future. The setbacks you've faced, the projects left unfinished, and the dreams you've put on hold – none of these are indicators of failure. Instead, they are chapters of your story that have yet to reach their climax, waiting for you to turn the page to success.

Your persistence in moving forward, your courage to face the challenges ahead, and your unshakable belief in your capabilities are what truly define you. They shape the essence of who you are and who you are destined to become. The path to achieving your dreams is paved with perseverance, with the understanding that success is not just a destination, but a journey filled with learning, growth, and endless possibilities.

Let this be your guiding principle: the only time you truly fail is when you stop trying. The moment you decide to give up is when your dreams start to fade into the realm of 'what could have been.' But as long as you keep moving and persist when faced with challenges, you are still on the path to success. Each step forward, no matter how small, is a step closer to realizing your dreams. Each obstacle overcome is a testament to your strength and resilience.

> *"The only time you truly fail is when you stop trying!"*

Embrace the knowledge that success is closer than you think. With every challenge you face, with every setback you overcome, you are sculpting the person you are meant to be. This journey of self-discovery and relentless pursuit of your goals shapes your character, hones your skills, and ultimately leads you to fulfill your aspirations.

So, as you close this book and look towards the horizon of your dreams, carry with you the lessons learned, the insights gained, and the undeniable belief in yourself. Remember, the road to completion is paved with persistence, and the only true failure is the failure to try.

Your journey does not end here. It is just the beginning. Armed with a newfound perspective, a resilient spirit, and the power of "yet," you are more prepared than ever to face the challenges ahead. The world is bursting with opportunities, waiting for you to seize them. So, take a deep breath, embrace the possibilities that lie before you, and step forward into the future with confidence and determination. The path ahead is yours to choose, and success is just around the corner. Keep moving forward, for you haven't failed; you're simply on your way to success. It's time to **Start the Finish!**

Closing Statement

I want to thank you for inviting me into your life, for dedicating your time and energy to this book, and for having the courage to finish what you started. Your commitment to this path of self-discovery and growth speaks to your strength and determination.

But remember, this journey doesn't end here, and neither does the impact of your actions. With the knowledge, insights, and resilience you've gained, you now have the power to transform not only your life but also to guide others on their own paths. I encourage you to take this newfound understanding and become a source of hope and encouragement to those who may feel weighed down by perceived failures or lost in uncertainty.

We are all connected in this complex reality of life. Each of us has faced setbacks, felt the sting of defeat, and questioned our path at some point. Yet, in these moments, we discover our true strength—not just as individuals but as a collective. By lifting each other up, sharing our stories of perseverance, and showing compassion, we can create a ripple effect of positive change that reaches far beyond ourselves.

As you move forward, spread the light of your resilience, share the wisdom you've gained, and be a source of strength for those who need it. Together, let's build a world where no one feels like a failure, where every setback is seen as an opportunity for growth, and where support and encouragement are always within reach.

Thank you once again for taking this journey with me. Your courage, your willingness to grow, and your potential to make a difference are truly inspiring. Let's continue to build each other up, knowing that each of us can be a light in the darkness, guiding the way toward a brighter, more resilient future.

May your path always shine with knowledge, courage, and compassion.

Reflective Exercises: Finishing What You Started

Objective: To guide you in revisiting a past endeavor you feel you failed at, helping you break down the journey into actionable steps, overcome obstacles, and ultimately complete what you started.

1. **Revisit a Past Endeavor**
   - **Identify Your Focus:** Reflect on a past project, goal, or endeavor you started but didn't complete.
   - **Understand the Impact:** Consider how not completing this task has impacted you, personally and professionally. Write down your thoughts, noting any feelings of regret, missed opportunities, or lessons learned.

2. **Reflect on Why You Stopped**
   - **Analyze Past Obstacles:** Take a moment to think about why you stopped pursuing this goal. Write down any external factors that may have played a role, such as lack of resources, time, or support. Then, consider the internal challenges you faced, like fear, self-doubt, or loss of motivation.
   - **Identify Patterns:** Notice if there are any recurring patterns in how you approach challenges or projects. Understanding these patterns can help you anticipate and overcome similar obstacles in the future.

3. **Reignite Your Motivation**
   - **Reconnect with Your 'Why':** Take some time to reflect on why you started this endeavor in the first place. What inspired you? What were your goals and dreams at the outset? Write down your initial motivations and how achieving this goal could positively impact your life now.

   - **Visualize Success:** Spend a few minutes visualizing what completing this goal would look and feel like. Imagine the satisfaction, pride, and opportunities that would come from achieving what you set out to do.

4. **Break Down the Goal**
   - **Set Clear Objectives:** Break down your goal into smaller, more manageable tasks. Identify what needs to be done and create a step-by-step plan to tackle each part. Make sure these tasks are specific and achievable.

   - **Prioritize and Schedule:** Prioritize these tasks based on their importance and the resources you have available. Set realistic deadlines for each task to keep yourself on track and motivated.

5. **Overcome Obstacles**
   - **Anticipate Challenges:** Consider the potential challenges you might face as you work towards completing your goal. Reflect on the obstacles that previously held you back and think about how you can overcome them this time around.

- **Create Solutions:** For each anticipated challenge, brainstorm possible solutions or strategies to address them. Whether it's seeking additional resources, building new skills, or developing a stronger support network, plan how you'll tackle each obstacle.

6. **Establish Accountability**
    - **Find Accountability Partners:** Identify someone who can support and hold you accountable as you work towards your goal. This could be a mentor, a friend, or a group with similar goals. Share your plan and progress with them regularly.
    - **Set Up Regular Check-Ins:** Schedule regular check-ins with your accountability partner(s) to review your progress, celebrate your achievements, and adjust your plan as needed.

7. **Stay Motivated and Resilient**
    - **Celebrate Small Wins:** Recognize and celebrate each milestone you reach, no matter how small. This will help maintain your motivation and remind you of the progress you're making.
    - **Practice Resilience:** When faced with setbacks, remind yourself that challenges are a natural part of any journey. Reflect on your past experiences and the strategies that have helped you overcome difficulties before.

8. **Reevaluate and Adapt**
   - **Review Your Progress:** Regularly evaluate your progress towards your goal. Are you meeting your deadlines? Are there any unexpected challenges that have arisen? Reflect on what's working and what needs adjustment.

   - **Adapt Your Plan:** Based on your progress and any new insights, adapt your plan as needed. Flexibility is key to staying on track, especially when circumstances change.

9. **Reflect on the Journey**
   - **Acknowledge Growth:** As you near the completion of your goal, take time to reflect on the personal growth you've experienced throughout this journey. How have you changed? What new skills or strengths have you developed?

   - **Commit to Future Goals:** Use the momentum and confidence you've gained from this process to commit to future goals. Reflect on how you can apply the lessons learned to other areas of your life.

Remember: As you engage with these reflective exercises, you're not just checking off tasks; you're creating a pathway to success that turns past setbacks into valuable lessons and key milestones. Each exercise brings you closer to realizing your dreams, proving that you have what it takes to achieve your goals. Stay committed, stay focused, and acknowledge that with every effort, you're building the future you envisioned. Keep going—you're closer than you think. You've got this!

About the Author

 Shawn Condra is passionate about helping others overcome challenges and realize their true potential. He understands what it feels like to be stuck or discouraged and is a firm believer in the power of resilience and the importance of never giving up on one's dreams.

 Shawn's journey has been shaped by personal experiences of navigating setbacks and finding the strength to move forward. He knows that life's challenges can be overwhelming, but he also believes that within each person lies the ability to rise above difficulties and create a path to success. This belief drives his commitment to helping others break free from limitations and embrace the opportunities that lie ahead.

 Beyond his writing, Shawn is a devoted husband to his wife, Stephany, and a proud father to his two daughters, Lillian and Abigail. Family is at the heart of everything Shawn does. Together with Stephany, he leads a children's ministry at their church, where they guide and mentor 3rd through 5th graders, helping them build a strong foundation of faith, character, and confidence. Shawn's work in ministry reflects his deep belief in the importance of nurturing the next generation with hope and resilience.

In his professional life, Shawn is guided by the same principles of care and support that define his personal life. His business motto, "Making Life Easier," is more than just a phrase—it's a commitment to simplifying and enhancing the lives of those he serves.

Shawn's life is centered on dedication, compassion, and a strong belief in the potential of every person. Whether through his business, his ministry, or his writing, he is committed to lifting others up, providing practical solutions, and making the journey through life a little easier. His goal is to encourage others to keep going and ensure that no one feels alone on their path to personal growth and fulfillment.

www.ingramcontent.com/pod-product-compliance
Lightning Source LLC
LaVergne TN
LVHW051844080426
835512LV00018B/3069